Votes at 16

Votes at 16

Youth Enfranchisement and the Renewal of American Democracy

Niall Guy Michelsen

LEXINGTON BOOKS

Lanham • Boulder • New York • London

Published by Lexington Books
An imprint of The Rowman & Littlefield Publishing Group, Inc.
4501 Forbes Boulevard, Suite 200, Lanham, Maryland 20706
www.rowman.com

6 Tinworth Street, London SE11 5AL, United Kingdom

British Library Cataloguing in Publication Information Available

Library of Congress Cataloging-in-Publication Data Available

ISBN 978-1-7936-1142-0 (cloth)
ISBN 978-1-7936-1144-4 (pbk)
ISBN 978-1-7936-1143-7 (electronic)

Contents

Introduction

This book follows a journey that began with a simple course assignment and ended with a proposal that could, over the long run, renew the problematic political status quo by generating a reinvigorated and engaged electorate that will be more representative of the general population than is currently the case. It began with a one-page reflection assignment on the question of whether we should let 16-year-olds vote. This evolved into an exploration of the arguments in favor of this idea. But it never amounted to much until I connected it with two other prominent features of our voting system. One is the decline of voting turnout rates over the last few decades. This has been attributed to the declining knowledge of and interest in politics of younger generations. The second is the inequality in voting across other demographic categories besides age. Of special importance is education. When we combine data about the differences of voting by age and by education, we discover that the decline in voting is concentrated among less educated citizens. College graduates continue to vote at strong levels. College attendance also exhibits an economic bias, with richer youth going to college at higher rates than poorer youth. This places the non-college youth at the center of attention with reform efforts. And, where are non-college youth found in abundance? In high school, which means that civics courses might be refashioned to focus on elections (primary, general, local, or state, it does not matter). The civics classes would help students pay many of the costs associated with voting (getting registered, finding out the voting site, etc.). And this would start new voters off in an environment when costs are low, thereby making it easier to begin the habit of voting. From this, just about all our young people would be assisted with voting the first time. This prominently includes young people unlikely to go to college.

1

In my journey down this path I have not found anything that puts the parts of the puzzle together in quite the way that I have. There are very different literatures that I am bridging. One is the growing literature on the political engagement (or lack thereof) of young citizens. Another is on political inequality and its causes. And yet another is literature on voting, which is voluminous. What makes this book unique is that I bridge these sub-fields and put together a coherent path that is both feasible and promises positive outcomes.

In many ways, this is an unusual story from the very beginning. My academic training in the discipline of Political Science is in the subfields of International Relations; Comparative Politics; and Political Theory. Over nearly 30 years of teaching in those areas, my teaching also extended into introductory courses for both political science and international studies. It was an introduction to political science course that initiated this project. Normally, academics follow their main research agenda with occasional forays into other subjects. Sometimes, and ideally frequently, research topics emerge as a product of teaching. Either the academic gets a Eureka moment while teaching a course or an untutored (and uncorrupted) student asks a simple question that the academic had never considered. This project came from the teaching side of my professional career, but it did not come from teaching in my primary field within the political science discipline. Moreover, when I first considered it, the idea seemed fanciful and it took a while before I began to take it seriously.

Even as that evolution was happening, I was acutely aware that it was what I call a little-l justice, meaning that while it engaged normative issues of right and wrong, the wrongs, were relatively minor. After all, the average 16–17-year-olds are not particularly interested in politics, and most of them will eventually grow up to become 18+ and thus become eligible to vote like the rest of us. Nonetheless, as time passed, my interest grew into excitement as I began to dig deeper into the topic and follow avenues of inquiry that took me to new and interesting places. Still my regular research projects that kept me busy outside of my teaching obligations were rooted in the IR/ Comparative fields. I maintained my interest in the topic and made my first professional presentation on the topic at a small conference in Spain. Much to my relief the audience did not ridicule me or laugh uproariously. Finally, I earned a semester to conduct research with no other professional obligations. With this opportunity to explore, I turned my attention to the voting age project to see if there was anything of legitimate interest.

So began a project focused on one specific aspect of American politics that was outside of my normal range of scholarship. Fortunately, colleagues have generously guided me through the considerable scholarship on elections and voting. Though this required considerable work, it may have also allowed me to view some of the connections with greater clarity, scholars who have invested years and decades into the subjects. I also hope there is some truth in the value of seeing the subject with fresh eyes.

An example of seeing connections that may have been missed by others is the two books that have been most pivotal in my evolution. Both are comparative in nature and my background in comparative politics doubtlessly aided me in studying them. Mark Franklin examined elections in 39 democracies since World War II, and this drew my attention to the negative consequences that came from dropping the voting age to 18, which occurred in the early 1970s in several countries. Aina Gallego drew my attention to the role that educational differences play in creating voting inequalities across the democratic world.

Of course, this work could not have been completed without the support of many supportive colleagues, friends, and one loving wife. I also want to thank Western Carolina University for granting me a semester free from teaching and service. Without that opportunity to dig into the massive literature on voting behavior, this project would have never taken off.

I want to give special thanks to some special people, beginning with Christopher Cooper who has provided intellectual and administrative support throughout the entire process. My Western Carolina University department colleagues handled me with respect, and not ridicule, when I presented an outline of the project to them, and for that I am very grateful. One thoughtful colleague said that he came into the presentation against the idea but I had changed his mind. Heidi Buchanan consistently provided valuable research assistance and moral support in her reference librarian role. And, thanks also to Dale Carpenter from Western Carolina University and local educator Jacob Buchanan who provided me useful information about how North Carolina school districts handle civics. Over the last few years, I have had the assistance of some graduate assistants helping with the research. Thanks for this go to Bryson Smith, Tyler Morrow, and Mollie Jones.

Special thanks go to John Mohler, a former graduate student from the 1990s who gallantly provided his advice, encouragement, and strong editing skills to each of the chapters. A few former colleagues from Roosevelt University, one of whom told me the work I was engaged in was important, deserve special mention for providing me moral support. The help from Mike Bryson, Jeff Edwards, and Mariano Magalhaes sustained me during some trying moments. A special thanks to Ginny Volio whose response a decade or so ago to a single question triggered this entire project. I would be remiss if I did not give thanks to the several anonymous seat mates on airplane flights, who served as captive audiences for my description of this book. Of course, a very special thanks to my lovely wife Terry Michelsen for her loving support. Without her steady encouragement and optimism this might well have remained uncompleted.

Chapter 1

Beginning Our Journey with a Single Question

SHOULD WE DROP THE VOTING AGE TO 16?

I posed this question to my Introduction to Political Science class a little more than a decade ago. It is the type of question that is intended to provoke thinking and discussion. I probably had seen something online that had triggered this assignment, though I cannot recall precisely. But I know that I simply wanted the students to go beyond their initial gut reactions, and begin thinking seriously about the criteria we use to determine voting eligibility. In other words, why are some citizens allowed to vote while the vote is denied to other citizens? The class and I batted the idea around, and since they rejected the proposal overwhelmingly, I played the role of advocate. Then I assigned the class a one-page reflection paper on the question of whether we should reduce the minimum voting age to 16. Only one student of the 20 or so in the class wrote a paper in favor of reducing the voting age to 16. The student admitted to initially rejecting the notion as crazy, but upon thinking about it some more, she changed her mind. A pedagogical success story! I encouraged her to submit an opinion piece to the nearest daily newspaper. It was accepted, and thankfully this was before the newspapers posted online comments, so she escaped the ire of the anticipated detractors.

From the outset, answers to this question fell into two predictable categories. *Yes,* they are intelligent enough, they pay taxes, and besides, it is their future, so they deserve the right to vote. *No,* they are immature, uninterested, and not ready for the responsibility of voting. By my unscientific estimation, the second (negative) response was the overwhelming majority. There are sound reasons for the initial negative reaction of many educated people, including my students. Some of these are supported by scholarship and point to evidence that youth below the age of 18 typically exhibit very low levels of interest in, or knowledge of, political matters. Some scholars question whether the youthful mind can handle such important and complex matters, and some even question whether adding this task onto the minds of youth could impair their cognitive development.[1] But after some reflection, those objections seemed to my student ally and me to be either silly in the extreme, or condescendingly discriminatory. The problem, as we saw it, is that this group is being judged by standards that we do not apply to the general population. No other demographic group (save immigrants) must demonstrate its interest in, and knowledge of, the basics of our political system. With that in mind, we managed to brush aside the skepticism of my colleagues and her classmates when we told them of our project. Recently the discussion has shifted in our direction to some degree.

A great deal of work has been going on to help prepare proto-citizens for citizenship. We can certainly put all the state civics requirements into this category. It is reported that all 50 states require some sort of civics/American government course as a condition of graduation. But only eight require any sort of statewide assessment of learning about our political system.[2] The variation across states with respect to the quality and rigor of the civics requirements mirrors another product of federalism, the voting rights in states.

Efforts to increase youth voting are underway in some states to allow age-ineligible students to pre-register to vote if they are close to the voting age. Some grade and high schools organize make-believe voting in an effort to begin nurturing citizenship skills and values. Currently, 16 states now allow 17-year-old citizens to vote in primary elections if they will be 18 when the general election comes around.[3]

The results are modest, with scholars reporting that students who participated in a pre-registration program voting are two or three percentage points higher than those who did not participate. So, this is not a magic elixir but still an improvement.[4] Just as importantly, scholars have reported that the positive impacts have been spread across the standard population categories: race, gender, political party. In fact, they found that the positive impact was stronger among African Americans and Hispanics than it was among Whites.[5] They attribute the positive impact to the fact that the pre-registration programs are embedded in high schools. This provides structure and support to the students and also makes the program available to students who might not be college-bound. The potential of this approach was so promising that the state of North Carolina's legislature banned the practice.[6] That law was overturned by the federal courts and now North Carolinian public school districts are required to provide registration materials to their students.[7]

Beginning this journey, I could not imagine that dropping the voting age would hold the potential to renew American democracy. By this, I mean that new and positive energy will be injected into the electoral system and in the process address some of the inequality that characterizes American voting patterns. But this recognition did not happen automatically and the ideas took time to germinate. I slowly reached the conclusion that this Votes at 16 reform had genuine merit. Then I found new and important reasons for supporting this reform.

Unbeknownst to us, some countries had already adopted Votes at 16. As we began our discussions only Cuba, Nicaragua, Brazil, and Austria had adopted Votes at 16.[8] And those countries were not seen as paragons of democratic virtue and were not considered to be models for mature democracies to mimic. Since then those countries have been joined by Ecuador, Argentina, and Malta along with several subnational jurisdictions.

In the United States this movement's momentum can be tracked along with some high-profile cases of individuals under the age of 18 gaining national and international acclaim. Though it did not spark a lot of grassroots agitating, the amazing decision to award the 17-year-old Malala Yousafzai the Nobel Peace Prize in 2014 laid the groundwork for the future.[9] Malala's courage, eloquence, and compassion are beyond the reach of most of us, of whatever age. But, recognizing that those heroic qualities could be exhibited by someone so young served to undermine the facile characterization of youth as less prepared to decide between Donald Trump and Hillary Clinton than the rest of America. The tragic shooting at Parkland High School in 2018 and the response it provoked lit a fire in the public mind about dropping the voting age to 16.[10] In 2019 *Time* Magazine anointed a 16-year-old woman who sailed across the Atlantic Ocean to address the United Nations on the issue of climate change as Person of the Year.[11] Greta Thunberg received extensive coverage, some of it laudatory and some of it derisive. While 16-year-old Jocelyn Wright did not cause a stir nationally when she started a petition (and generating 43,000 signatures) in opposition to abortion legislation in her home state of Alabama, her actions demonstrate that beyond the headlines, young citizens who are not able to vote have been motivated to take actions available to them.[12]

These examples, except for Malala's, were all in hotly contested issues that American politics and society seem unable to resolve. Gun control, climate change, and abortion are all hot-button political issues. Perhaps the youth can help where we have failed. Malala's campaign to bring universal education to women in Pakistan does not fall into that category but nearly everyone applauded her goal of bringing education to Pakistani women. Americans agree with the Parkland students in opposing school shootings and favoring some type of gun control.[13] Greta Thunberg's powerful presence and address fit easily into a vigorous partisan fight in the United States and around the world. Although some questioned her competence, most recognized that the issue she gave voice to was an important one and, that it had motivated a young person like her to lead the charge, seems entirely fitting. Evidence shows that young people generally support environmental protection more than older generations.[14] The same can be said about abortion rights, with 60 percent of women and 61 percent of men agreeing that abortion should be available in all or most cases.[15] On the other side, there are, of course, very strident opponents.

Scattered across the country, some local jurisdictions are changing or discussing changing the voting age to 16. In 2013, Takoma Park in Maryland adopted Votes at 16 for their elections, marking the first American jurisdiction to do so. Their imagination was stirred by the debate within Scotland about who would be eligible to vote in their upcoming 2014 referendum on independence.[16] Following Takoma Park's lead, local elections have been opened to 16–17-year-olds in Greenbelt and Hyattsville (both also in Maryland), with Berkeley, California, opening school board elections to 16–17-year-olds.[17] It has been reported that three states and the District of Columbia are considering dropping the voting age to 16, with the goal of opening it up for federal elections as well as local elections.[18] In early 2019 the new Democratic majority in the House of Representatives proposed an amendment to reduce the voting age to 16, but it failed by a wide margin (126–305), without even carrying a majority of Democrats.[19] Andrew Yang, whose candidacy for the Democratic presidential nomination had surprised many with its ability to overcome a lack of political experience and name recognition, has embraced Votes at 16.[20]

Behind the headlines, scholars have also been warming to this possibility, and have been reporting some intriguing results. The first scholar to draw attention to the positive possibilities to dropping the voting age to 16 was Mark Franklin.[21] Hart and Atkins were among the first to come out in support of the Votes at 16 concept, publishing a still valuable work in 2011.[22] In the past year, Hart and Youniss listed reducing the voting age as one of their most important keys to capturing the political energy and excitement of youth.[23] Numerous scholars have joined in the effort with many focusing on the second wave of countries, especially in the case of Austria.[24] While not advocating Votes at 16, Gallego drew attention to the educational divide that characterizes voting patterns worldwide.[25] These and other advocates claim that this change will increase the voting turnout rates. In this book, I show that over the long term, it can do more than that. In fact, it might lead to a more representative electorate that will include larger numbers of non-college, working-class Americans.

Critics maintain that if voting is central to the functioning of a healthy democracy, then extending the vote to uneducated and uninterested voters seems contrary to common sense. Rather than strengthening the quality of democracy, this would weaken it by adding voters who do not care about politics and do not know about the political system or issues. This logic, however, is not consistently applied to currently eligible voters. It is somewhat specious to quibble over the amount of political knowledge or the degree of political sophistication of potential voters in light of how poorly existing voters rank on these scores.

Two recent scholars have concluded that average voters, not just the youngest voters, do not possess very much political knowledge.[26] Achen and Bartels' survey of political science research on these matters makes a compelling case that average voters know alarmingly little about politics and government and average citizens tend to agree to the positions adopted by their preferred political party rather than reaching conclusions on the basis of their own analyses. Nonetheless, it is incumbent upon us to preserve as much of the representative democratic ideals as we can. And if something is proposed that threatens to reduce the existing political quality, we should reject it. Certainly no one favors adding to the voting rolls large numbers of essentially random voters.

Interestingly, being a member of a fully enfranchised group seems to nearly immunize a person from ever being barred from voting for any reason with only a couple of exceptions. Across the 50 American states, the most common reason to remove someone's right to vote is due to felony conviction.[27] The second largest cause of someone losing the right to vote is by a judge declaring someone "incompetent."[28] Other than that, once a group gains the franchise there are few mechanisms to determine when someone in that group does not have the ability to discern basic political facts. This threatens to undermine the main arguments against reducing the voting age. If a lack of political knowledge is not a reason to take away someone's voting rights, how can it be a reason to deny to an entire large group of people the right to vote because many of them do not have the requisite political sophistication? Rights to vote are granted to groups (women for instance) and are taken away from individuals (typically felons).

Back to our journey: the student and I had already heard several versions of the slippery slope arguments—would we support 10-year-olds voting? Consequently, we took up the basic questions of (1) can teenagers at that age make informed decisions and (2) would they be interested in politics and voting? These are two very different questions, but scholarly critics typically point out the deficiencies of young cohorts on both counts. We asked ourselves what were the qualities that eligible voters possess that the 16–17-year-olds do not. One of the most common claims involves the lack of political knowledge. Nearly all criticisms of reducing the voting age point to the gap in political knowledge, with older Americans demonstrating much more knowledge than younger Americans. On its face this is hardly a surprising fact. In all honesty, who among us would deny that our younger selves did not know as much as we know now. The same is true with driving skills—those skills, like political knowledge, tend to grow with age.

So, while this criticism rings true when first introduced, we also recognize that it is not the case that 16–17-year-olds have zero political knowledge and that the youngest 18+ age group has a great deal of political knowledge. Instead there is a sliding scale, with quite a few college-bound 16–17-year-olds possessing a great deal of political knowledge and quite a few of the youngest 18+ age group with very little political knowledge. The two populations overlap, they are not exclusive. Hence the saying, "If you let stupid old people vote, why don't you let smart young people vote?"

So, it is not that one group totally lacks political knowledge (or driving skills), it is that on average younger voters have insufficient political knowledge (driving skills). Some discussions seem to suggest that at age 18 a magical transformation happens, sort of like a caterpillar changing into a butterfly. In this case, it is an awkward and befuddled proto-citizen that transfigures into a beautiful citizen, with all the qualities this implies. Certainly, the teen years are characterized by dramatic changes both physical and mental. In reality, if there is a marked jump in political knowledge at ages beginning at 18, it is better explained by the magical effect of being allowed to vote at 18. Thus, it is a social decision, rather than a physiological change that creates this gap. Think again of a 15-year-old who is not allowed to start the car ignition and who cannot parallel park, in comparison to a 16-year-old who has been allowed to drive the car and has practiced parallel parking. It is engaging with the real activity that generates interest/skill, not reading about it in a book.

In a widely cited article Chan and Clayton threw cold water on efforts in the United Kingdom in the early 2000s to lower the voting age to 16.[29] In one part of their argument they rejected the standard criticism that since younger voters are expected to vote at lower levels than other age groups, they should not be allowed to vote. They sensibly argued that whether the youth vote at high or low levels has no impact on any other voters. So, when you do not bother to vote, it does absolutely no harm to my vote (if anything it confers more power on my vote). They also maintained that any loss in the overall voting rate must be balanced against the psychological benefit accruing to those youth who would be allowed to vote.

On the other hand, they were very concerned by the expected lack of political knowledge that this new group would bring to the ballot booths. In this case, your ill-informed and random vote negates my well-researched and wise vote. To support their claims, Chan and Clayton reported on survey data that suggested that 16–17-year-olds are both less interested and less knowledgeable about politics than older voters, including 18–19-year-olds. Their interest level data does show a significant pattern with interest growing as age increases. And the level of interest for the youngest is very low indeed.

In an important sense, Chan and Clayton hold youngest voters to a standard that many eligible voters cannot meet. So, while Chan and Clayton's criticisms are reasonable, these charges can be made against the existing voters who also exhibit very limited political knowledge. Nonetheless, they and other critics are correct, that younger voters are less informed than older voters. At least this is true when the younger group lacks official voting rights.

One feature of this seminal critical work is worth noting, and was noticed by the authors themselves.

> Now, we know that sixteen and seventeen-year-olds are especially uninterested in politics, but we also know that over the next several years of their lives, they go through a remarkable period of political awakening. Do we want our young voters to develop a habit of not voting when they are not interested in politics?[30]

They accurately point out that the beginning of a voter's mature life is critical, and thus, so is the age and circumstances at first vote. This warning ignores the evidence that currently too few young people are developing the habit of voting under the 18-year-old voting rule. As research findings from Latin America and Europe have begun to show, there is a fundamental difference in levels of interest and knowledge when groups can vote as opposed to when the groups are not allowed to vote. It is natural that when voting is something in the distant future (and to 16-year-olds 2 years is a very long time) there is little incentive to acquire political knowledge. In other words, "Such knowledge is simply not as relevant to them as it is to their older and eligible peers."[31]

EMPIRICAL EVIDENCE FROM COUNTRIES WITH VOTES AT 16

Having discussed these questions in theoretical terms, it is now time to turn to the empirical evidence that has been accumulated thus far. Without evidence, we are condemned to compare two distinct populations. The first population includes those who became eligible to vote at 18, and the second includes those who are too young to vote. Missing are those who became eligible to vote at 16. As we will see, there are reasons to believe that being categorized as fit, or unfit, to vote seems to have an impact on how someone views politics and voting. If we can establish that 16–17-year-olds behave in much the same way as other voters behave, then the plausibility of this reform is bolstered. It will still leave the question of whether it is a good idea for the United States but that will have to wait for further chapters. Now, on to the evidence.

This option was not open to my student and me because the scholarship on this topic was only in its infancy. However, since Chan and Clayton's article was published and provided a scholarly basis for critics, new scholarly evidence has emerged from data generated by elections in which 16–17-year-olds were eligible to vote. The question becomes whether 16–17-year-olds exhibit the political maturity to act as responsible voters. This has two components. One is the voter turnout rates of those who gained the right to become a voter at age 16, in comparison to others who only earned that right at age 18. The second component is how coherent their voting is. For example, do they vote for the party that is closest to them in ideological terms? Both forms of data are available by using either survey data where citizens are asked to describe their voting behavior or by official data supplied by the government. Success is typically measured by impact on turnout rates, especially of the youngest cohorts, and by assessing the quality of the voting done by those citizens.[32] It is important to keep in mind that voting is not the only goal of efforts to reform political processes. As Henry Milner informs us, voting is a means toward the goal of engaged citizenship.[33]

In 2020 an extremely timely book was published whose goal it was to capture the current state of knowledge drawn from elections where 16-year-olds have been allowed to vote.[34] The book contains valuable case studies that supplement the journal articles on this topic that have been appearing in the last 5–10 years. But its greatest value is that it represents the beginning of a truly comparative type of analysis of this subject. The case studies and other articles provide the data for those comparisons.

When looking at cases where elections have been opened to 16–17-year-olds we must recognize that not all elections are equal. Some countries have opened all their elections to the 16–17-year-olds. Other countries open some elections at the municipal or state level to 16–17-year-olds while leaving other elections only open to those 18 years or older. For example, it is commonplace for national governments to allow, but not require some of the municipal or state governments to implement Votes at 16. This creates opportunities to compare across very similar political systems that vary only on whether they have Votes at 16 or not.

These real-world experiments and permanent changes permit a valuable opportunity to test the social scientific hypotheses generated by Chan and Clayton and others. Strident critics would predict that due to their lack of political knowledge and low political interest these new voters would vote at significantly lower rates than the 18–19-year-olds age group. Less strident critics would anticipate that their voting rates would marginally extend the downward trend which extends from high-turnout old voters to low-turnout young voters. This pessimism is rooted in the well-documented record of continuing decline in voting rates with young voters having the lowest voting rates of all. Optimists would predict that the new voters would match or at least approach the levels of the youngest 18+ age group in both voting turnout and political sophistication. This optimism is rooted in the work done in 2004 by Mark Franklin, which argued that 18 is a particularly bad age to begin voting.[35]

In 2020 Franklin conducted a statistical analysis of the data that has become available about elections in the 7 countries that have opened up all their elections to 16–17-year-old voters. Not all elections have comparable data, or data at all. From the states that have had sufficient elections (three for survey data and two for official data), Franklin reached two significant conclusions. First, he concluded that the claim that advocates make on the positive impact of reducing the voting age on voting rates has been realized. At the same time, however, he noted that there is evidence that young voters exhibit a high amount of volatility. By this he meant that the youngest voters do not have stable party affiliations. Consequently, they shift from one party to another much more readily than do older voters. This is not surprising because it is known that the newest voters are less entrenched in the habit of voting overall, and in their party allegiance. They are also most susceptible to changes in voting rules. Critics of this reform will note that this is evidence that young voters are not politically sophisticated and are thus more likely to respond to cheap promises. In this sense, this represents a decrease in the coherence of the election.[36] We will now look at the specific cases where 16–17-year-olds are eligible to vote.

A quick look shows that the cases came into existence in different ways and in very different political contexts. With respect to instances of full voting rights we have information on five Latin American countries and Austria. For partial voting rights cases, we have four other European cases as well as the United States. Latin American countries were the earliest national governments to adopt Votes at 16.[37] They also remain the most numerous among those countries who have fully adopted this age reform. Cuba led the way with adoption occurring after a referendum in 1976. Nicaragua followed in 1984 under the Sandinista government. Brazil lowered its voting age to 16 in 1988, and voting is compulsory (but not for citizens 16–17 or over 70). Ecuador followed in 2008 using a referendum to approve this change. Argentina, which also has compulsory voting, followed suit and dropped the minimum voting age to 16 in 2012.[38] Austria had experimented with Votes at 16 in some municipal elections and made the move to full voting rights in 2007, becoming the first, and until 2018, only European country adopting this full reform. Malta became the second European to adopt Votes at 16 in 2018 but there is no scholarship on how the change has impacted elections. Several European countries (Germany, Norway, Scotland, and Estonia) and

Table 1.1   Case Studies of Votes at 16

Country	All Elections?	Some Elections?	Began?	Other
Cuba	Yes	Tested in one Province in 1973	1978	Scores low on Democracy Indexes
Nicaragua	Yes		1984	Part of "democratization" process
Brazil	Yes		1988	Compulsory, but not for 16–17-year-olds
Austria	Yes	Municipal elections began in 2005	2007	First European
Ecuador	Yes		2008	Compulsory, but not for 16–17-year olds
Argentina	Yes		2012	Only Latin American country with youngest the most left
Malta			2018	No data yet
Germany		Yes	1996	Some German states (Lander) adopt Votes at 16
Norway	Yes	Yes	2011	Complicated initial election due to terrorist attack
United States		Yes	2013	Some states allow local governments to adopt Votes at 16, some states do not
Scotland		Yes	2014 (Independence Referendum)	In 2015 all Scottish elections opened to 16–17-year-olds
Estonia		Yes	2017	Part of democratization reforms

Source: Based upon data published in Eichhorn, Jan, and Johannes Bergh, eds., 2020.

the United States have experimented with reduced voting age but have not yet totally embraced the Votes at 16 reform.

Among the proto-citizenship elections, the case of the 2014 Scottish independence referendum holds a special place. It is impressive, and an indication of the growing interest in youth voting, that during an election determining the identity of Scotland itself, they chose to experiment with lowering the voting age to 16. Based on a survey of 14–17-year-olds done in 2013 a year before the referendum, the Scottish youth appeared to be leaning toward voting in a direction that was not determined by how their parents leaned or their school.[39] Instead, it appears that they, like other voters, were influenced by positions and arguments advocated by external actors, but they made their choices independently. After the referendum and the strong showing of the 16–17-year-old cohort, the voting age was dropped to 16 for all elections in Scotland. Subsequent elections show that the high level of interest demonstrated by the 16–17-year-olds, that could have been attributable to the high-profile referendum, has been maintained.[40] These strong results hold up when the young Scots are compared to their age-cohorts in the rest of the United Kingdom where 16–17-year-olds are not allowed to vote. Scottish youth demonstrate much higher levels of political interest and faith in the political system. Moreover, there is evidence that youth are influencing the older generations on political matters.[41]

In Norwegian elections since 2011 the youngest voters have exhibited very strong turnout rates. The confluence of a terrorist attack in 2011 along with the 16–17-year-old voting trial made it challenging to disentangle the impact of the two events. This has been termed a "dynamic generational mobilization" and has been seen from 2011 to 2017.[42] German states (Lander) have been experimenting with Votes at 16 in some state and municipal elections since 1996. The value of having some states experimenting with the lower voting age while others do not, is that it allows us to compare the behavior of voters across different election rules. An interesting case is Estonia, which faced a lot of fundamental political questions as it emerged from its Communist past. It was around 2012 that they began considering dropping the voting age from 21 to 18. Perhaps because the reform was seen considering other recent developments dedicated to extending and securing full democracy, but the parliamentary debates were not hotly contested. Ultimately the national parliament approved a law that opened local elections to the 16–17-year-old cohort. This happened in 2017, so there is not much reliable evidence on the impact of this reform on those elections. Results from the United States' local elections in which Votes at 16 was operative reflect some of the same patterns seen elsewhere with the 16–17-year-olds outvoting the general public in the local elections.[43] Although elites were required to bring these into effect, the role of young people in speaking eloquently on behalf of the reform should not be overlooked.

There are seven major takeaways from the case studies that are currently available. These cases have many idiosyncratic features, but here we are only interested in those that relate to the possibility of instituting Votes at 16 in the United States. All these points have been made in the context of more than one electoral system, and some of them have been raised in virtually every case that has been analyzed. The first point relates to the origins of Votes at 16 in the different locations. Where this reform has been put into practice it has almost always been with parties of the Left being its champions. This is expected as Conservative or Right parties tend to resist reforms unless they are modest and not expected to disrupt the status quo. Conversely, parties of the Left typically seek to bring into the political arena disenfranchised groups. Humbly, I will claim that this reform will be modest but will also bring into the political arena groups whose participation has been declining. There is one note of concern involving the Washington, D.C., city council that took up the issue. Even though the city is heavily Democratic, which is typically a key ingredient in successful efforts to gain approval, it never received approval. The lesson is that even when popular sentiments seem to be in alignment the machinations of politics can intervene to prevent approval.[44]

The second point is that those Left parties hope to get rewarded by the 16–17-year-old voters and, in some places, it seems they are rewarded. Among Latin American countries, only in Argentina are the youngest voters farther to the Left than the older voters. In Europe, the balance seems to be the reverse, with the youngest voters being Left-leaning and more interested in smaller or third parties, especially the Greens. In Estonia, the decision of the political parties to support or not support lowering the voting age had an impact on the votes cast by the newest voters.[45] This is very important for the pragmatic reason that it, in conjunction with the first point, confirms the fears of the Conservative parties that they will lose electorally under this reform.

Third, the youngest voters show the volatility that Franklin noted. This should not come as a surprise due to the fact that first-time voters must figure out their own political preferences first and then determine how those fit into the local political situation. This takes a lot of effort the first time, and thereafter it gets easier. Partly it gets easier because as one chooses a party and votes accordingly for a few elections it becomes standard behavior not requiring periodic reconsiderations. Research has shown that between the ages of 14 and 25 political interest tends to increase before it levels off at what is considered the mature level.[46] Bergh reported results from the 2011 Norwegian election that contradict or challenge those who say enfranchisement increases political interest, and who say that 16–17-year-olds are politically mature in terms of having stable political perspectives.[47] Those elections were municipal elections that were experimenting with Votes at 16, so that group of voters were not endowed with complete suffrage.

However, there is evidence that after a few elections the young citizens begin to stabilize around a preferred party before long so the volatility is not a permanent condition. Austrian results revealed that youngest voters show a tendency to the more extreme parties, but move to the center and stabilize their party preferences.[48] This should offer some solace to Conservatives because it indicates that young voters are open to recruitment, and are not fixed in the Left camp forever. Thus, the volatility that Mark Franklin found might be a temporary condition and not a harbinger for a life of rapidly switching parties.

Fourth, one of the most important elements is that it is often the youth who have characteristics of low likelihood of voting that benefit most from Votes at 16. This point was made explicitly in the case of Scotland with class differences in terms of levels of political engagement largely disappearing.[49] And it was also noted by a scholar whose long-term interest has been in the political dropouts, Henry Milner. In his overview of the Votes at 16 landscape, Milner discusses the necessity of connecting the voting reform to civic education and makes the following observation about the impact of civics: "civic education has the largest effect on young Americans with less exposure to political information."[50] This will be very important to this book, because it represents the key to what takes this reform from little-j justice to Big-J Justice.

Fifth, another important point to emerge from these cases is the significance of civic education in preparing the 16–17-year-olds to play their proper role in elections. This point was made several times which underlines its importance if this reform is to bear the fruit its advocates envision. When Estonia adopted the reform, they also recognized that it places a heavy burden of civic education, and the analysts have found that it seems that they have determined a way to provide neutral civic education, thereby avoiding political controversy.[51]

Sixth, the impact of voting at 16 has two psychological impacts of note. One is the impact of voting rights on the young person. The other is the sense of faith and optimism that young people tend to bring to the political arena. A 16–17-year-old citizen can fall into one of three categories in terms of their right to vote. They can be ineligible to vote due to their excessive youth. Or, they can be eligible to vote in some elections (typically local elections) but not eligible to vote in some elections (typically national elections). Here society is effectively saying, "We do not trust you to vote on the important matters, but we will let you vote on lesser matters to see if you are going to break something." Finally, the 16–17-year-old citizen might be eligible to vote in all elections.

These categories are significant because the decision whether to vote and how seriously to take the right to vote can vary depending on the status of the voter. The point is that each category generates distinct psychological characteristics. The first category provides little motivation for the person to pay attention to government and politics. The second and third categories contain significant motivations for its members to learn about the political system and the major issues of the day. We therefore expect members of the latter two categories to have greater political knowledge than the first. Instead of being passive observers of politics, they become engaged citizens with much greater interest in politics. This is true for those with both full and partial voting rights, but it is much more the case with full voting rights. And this is what is reported. Another way of saying this is that studies evaluating levels of political sophistication among 16–17-year-olds must specify whether those citizens possess full voting rights or not.

However, the latter two categories differ in a significant way. The members of the third category who have complete voting rights have a good chance of developing into engaged citizens who vote in nearly every election going forward. This is only true, however, if they begin voting when they become eligible. By contrast, the second category whose members have only partial voting rights might feel either confused by their mixed status, disrespected by society, or a combination of both. There is reason to be concerned that those in this category might not develop into engaged citizenship because of this anomalous situation.

Advocates of Votes at 16 should appreciate that Scotland opened up their independence referendum vote to 16–17-year-olds and they performed so admirably that all Scottish elections were opened up to them. But because Scotland is a member of the United Kingdom, those 16–17-year-olds cannot vote in the UK elections. While this would only be temporary, as they would have to wait no longer than two years to reach the age of 18, it could discourage some youth and act as a barrier in the development of the voting habit. While the numbers impacted by this might not be high, it is worth considering since at that age they are most subject to change. A second valuable psychological point that is often overlooked is that the youngest voters tend to be the most optimistic and have the highest opinions of political parties and, in some but not all cases, of the government itself.[52] At this time in world history there are probably no political systems that could not benefit from the injection of some optimism. Moreover, the youngest voters demonstrated greater satisfaction with political parties and parliaments, but they had less satisfaction with the governments. Satisfaction with the core democratic institutions is important because it provides legitimacy for the political system.[53] The Latin American evidence shows that those who began voting at 16 expressed greater political satisfaction than those who began voting at later ages.

Seventh and finally, the most important outcome is the prevalence of 16–17-year-olds outperforming the youngest 18+ age group. As has been noted by others, even graphs used by the critics Chan and Clayton show the same pattern.[54] The quality of the vote as measured by congruence between the voter's beliefs and the candidate or party they voted for was equal to that of older voters.[55] These results combine to paint a clear picture that young voters, when given an opportunity to join their elders on an equal basis, demonstrate the same or higher levels of interest than their immediate elders.[56]

Norwegian elections since their first with Votes at 16, in 2011, saw higher than expected turnout by young voters suggesting that the terrorist attack in Norway in 2011 had a positive effect on mobilizing these voters and that it left an impression on folks long after the event itself. As that terrorist attack moved further in the past, the effect on the youngest citizens remained stronger than on older generations. This is not surprising because older generations are fixed into their habits whereas younger generations can more easily move into or move out of electoral politics. That also indicates that this is partly a result of a life-cycle process in which those who are at home living with parents have a higher likelihood of developing a voting habit than are those who are not living with their family.[57]

Austria, which has high turnout rates normally, has not exhibited any decline among those who began voting at 16 in comparison to those who began voting at 18. Eva Zeglovits examined results from two Austrian cities early in the period of full citizenship for 16–17-year-olds. In each case the 16–17-year-old age group voted at higher rates and demonstrated equal political sophistication.[58] Evidence also comes from local German elections in which 16–17-year-olds turned out at higher rate than 18–24-year-olds.[59] A researcher concluded that in the case of Germany, "If turnout is indeed habit forming as the extant research strongly suggests, that higher turnout of young first-time voters will result in a higher number of habitual voters."[60]

CONCLUSION

This chapter has advanced two fundamental points. The first is that many of the initial criticisms of Votes at 16 cannot be easily maintained. Thus, some 16-year-olds are smart enough and mature enough to cast responsible votes, while some senior citizens fail on both counts. Yet, only they, the older citizens, are allowed to vote.

If the first point tackled the negative case against Votes at 16, the second point made the affirmative case in favor of this reform. Compelling evidence from Latin America and Europe has shown that the 16–17-year-olds outperform the youngest 18+ age group. Thus, rather than detracting from the quality of our elections, they would contribute positively to it. In the words of the editors of a recent book, "While we cannot conclusively say whether the implementation of Votes at 16 resulted in positive changes in every instance, we have little evidence to suggest that it has been detrimental in the cases studied."[61] Researchers concluded, "In sum, lowering the voting age does not appear to have a negative impact on input legitimacy and the quality of democratic decisions."[62]

While this speaks well for lowering the voting age to 16, it raises another question: why does the youngest 18+ age group not vote or otherwise appear as politically engaged as their younger cohorts? We will need to understand both sides of that coin. Just as we have maintained that attaining the age of 18 does not correspond to suddenly becoming interested and active in politics, we should not err in the opposite direction and conclude that at 18 people suddenly lose interest in politics and become politically disengaged. Something else must be going on.

The reasons for this are not yet clear. The most popular explanation among scholars is that the youngest voters tend to live in a much more conducive social setting than do the slightly older voters.[63] The youngest tend to still be at home and around parents who are likely to be voters, whereas the slightly older ones tend to spend most of their time among other young non-voters. That explanation is based on Mark Franklin's observation that any other age between 15 and 24 would be preferable to 18 at which to begin voting.[64]

Another factor contributing to this could be what has been called the novelty effect.[65] Voting for the first time might seem like a unique and fun experience and an act recognizing their status as an adult, and having done that once, the young voter might not find the second time as exciting. Another possibility, and one that does not exclude the first, is referred to as the Hawthorne effect in which the fact that one is being closely observed affects the subject's behavior.[66] This works since society in general, the media, and especially political parties will pay a great deal of attention to the behavior of the newly enfranchised groups. In combination, the novelty of voting plus knowing the whole world is watching should motivate these new voters to turn out. While we cannot draw firm conclusions regarding the reasons for the strong turnout numbers for 16–17-year-olds and lower numbers for the youngest 18+ age group we can conclude that voting in a single election is incapable of establishing a habit of voting.

Another point derived from these cases is that simply granting the right to vote changes the young person. It is important to recognize that being granted the right to vote, either fully or partially, has an effect of transforming the recipient. Changing from being an observer to a participant has an impact. This has also been shown in the effect that civics classes have on proto-voters. In other words, if you want to make them citizens, do not treat them like apprentice citizens, treat them like citizens, let them vote.

At this point of the journey I was thinking of the issue in terms of little-j justice. After all, compared to the injustices in the political arena facing African Americans, women, Native Americans, and drafted soldiers in an unpopular war, the plight of 16- and 17-year-old citizens seems paltry in comparison. In a couple of years, they would be able to vote, so while justice delayed is justice denied, it is denied only for two years. Compare that with the African Americans who could not become White; the women who could not become men; the Native Americans who could not become White; and the draftees who might not return from Vietnam alive. Today's 16- and 17-year-olds have a very high probability of surviving to the age of 18 and will be welcomed with open arms by the full citizenry. Most of the advocates of dropping the voting age to 16 base the entirety of their arguments in the little-j justice realm. That is, they typically mention that many in this age group work, and all pay taxes, and they are given the right to drive automobiles. Furthermore, they have energy and bring new issues to the table.

We had concluded that the arguments against dropping the voting age were somewhat arbitrary and that the evidence thus far belies those harsh evaluations. Sixteen- and Seventeen-year-olds are only marginally less knowledgeable than the rest of us. They will not vote if they are not interested. We do not do such a great job voting in numbers, and voting wisely. There is no reason why dropping the voting age to 16 must lead to Votes at 14 or 12, etc. The problem is that many adults know 16-year-olds and doubt their wisdom. College students have younger brothers/sisters who seem incapable of logical thought. We all have memories of our own youthful selves and our immature and sometimes silly thoughts. But (1) none of that disqualifies adults, and (2) this caricature is belied by examples of youth behaving bravely and clear-eyed.

Now, the task in front of us seemed insurmountable (an amendment to the US Constitution). As a political scientist, I understood how difficult it is for two individuals without any discernible political power to make a fundamental change in a huge political system. At the same time, I had also been an observer of massive political changes that occurred with great rapidity and without the benefit of being long predicted. Two of these are the end of the Cold War, and the reversal of elite and popular opinion on Gay Marriage. Most students might also add the progress made on the legalization of marijuana as another case.

Notwithstanding the points established thus far, skeptics could fairly argue that even if some 16–17-year-olds are prepared to make positive political contributions, and even if some Latin American and European countries are comfortable with Votes at 16, this does not automatically mean that it is right for the United States. Though we cannot yet conclude that this reform is proper for the United States, the following chapters attempt to make this clear.

Chapter 2 looks at the history of suffrage in the United States to show that this reform is consistent with our political history. It also surveys the current political landscape to establish the case that if some reforms can be made, it might serve us well. Chapter 3 focuses on political inequality that exists in the United States (and nearly everywhere) which famously says the electoral chorus sings with an upper-class accent. It specifically points out how that inequality afflicts the least educated among us. Chapter 4 explores how voting becomes, or does not become, a habit. This makes the case for the Big-J Justice claim that I make. It completes the section of the book where the case is made for why this particular reform makes sense. Chapter 5 then delves into how this reform might come into existence broadly if not universally, in the United States. It discusses the pivotal role that civics courses in the high schools can be expected to play when Votes at 16 comes into existence. Chapter 6 wraps up the book and makes some projections about the expected impact of lowering the voting age on the 2016 and future national elections.

With that in mind we will now turn our attention to two vital aspects of the story. The first is to place this proposed change in the composition of the electorate into the longer historical context of American politics. The second is to confront some of the problems with American democracy that are in full bloom currently, but that have been around for a long while.

NOTES

1. Dawkins, Richard, and R Elisabeth Cornwell. "Dodgy Frontal Lobes, y'dig?: The Brain Just Isn't Ready to Vote at 16." *The Guardian*, December 13, 2003. https://www.theguardian.com/politics/2003/dec/13/highereducation.voterapathy

2. Brennan, Jan, and Hunter Railey. "The Civics Education Initiative 2015-17." Education Trends. *Education Commission of the States*, September, 2017. https://www.ecs.org/wp-content/uploads/The-Civics-Education-Initiative-2015-2017.pdf

3. "Voting in Primaries at 17 Years Old." News Organization. *Ballotpedia*, April 30, 2019. https://ballotpedia.org/Voting_in_primaries_at_17_years_old

4. McDonald, Michael P., and Matthew Thornburg. "Registering the Youth through Voter Preregistration." *New York University Journal of Legislation & Public Policy* 13 (2010): 551–72.

5. Holbein, John B., and D. Sunshine Hillygus. "Making Young Voters: The Impact of Preregistration on Youth Turnout." *American Journal of Political Science* 60, no. 2 (April 2016): 364–82.

6. Blythe, Anne. "Elimination of NC Voter Preregistration Program Creates Confusion for DMV and Elections Officials." *The Charlotte Observer*, July 3, 2014. https://www.charlotteobserver.com/news/politics-government/article9137564.html

7. Holbein, John B., and D. Sunshine Hillygus. *Making Young Voters: Converting Civic Attitudes into Civic Action*, 176. Cambridge, UK: Cambridge University Press, 2020.

8. Petraca, Constanza Sanhueza. "Does Voting at a Younger Age Have an Effect on Satisfaction with Democracy and Political Trust? Evidence from Latin America." In *Lowering the Voting Age to 16: Learning from Real Experiences Worldwide*, 103–19. Palgrave Studies in Young People and Politics. Palgrave Macmillan, 2020.

9. "Malala Yousafzai Biographical." Organizational. The Nobel Peace Prize. Accessed March 7, 2020. https://www.nobelprize.org/prizes/peace/2014/yousafzai/biographical/

10. Mazzei, Patricia. "Parkland: A Year After the School Shooting That Was Supposed to Change Everything." *New York Times*, February 13, 2019. https://www.nytimes.com/2019/02/13/us/parkland-anniversary-marjory-stoneman-douglas.html

11. Alter, Charlotte, Suyin Haynes, and Justin Worland. "Time 2019 Person of the Year — Greta Thunberg." *Time*, December 23, 2019. https://time.com/person-of-the -year-2019-greta-thunberg/

12. Gray, Emma. "Here's What It's Like To Be A Teenage Girl In Alabama Right Now." *News. Huffington Post: Women*, May 23, 2019. https://www.huffpost.com/ entry/teen-girl-alabama-abortion-ban-jocelyn-wright_n_5ce6a9f6e4b0547bd1337c2e

13. Schaeffer, Katherine. "Share of Americans Who Favor Stricter Gun Laws Has Increased since 2017." *Research Organization. Pew Research Center*, October 16, 2019. https://www.pewresearch.org/fact-tank/2019/10/16/share-of-americans-wh o-favor-stricter-gun-laws-has-increased-since-2017/

14. Pew Research Center. "After Seismic Political Shift, Modest Changes in Public's Policy Agenda." *Research Organization. Pew Research Center*, January 24, 2017. https://www.people-press.org/2017/01/24/after-seismic-political-shift-modest -changes-in-publics-policy-agenda/

15. Pew Research Center. "Public Opinion on Abortion: Views on Abortion 1995-2019." *Polling Organization. Religion and Public Life*, August 29, 2019. https://ww w.pewforum.org/fact-sheet/public-opinion-on-abortion/

16. Douglas, Joshua A. "Lowering the Voting Age from the Ground Up: The United States' Experience in Allowing 16-Year-Olds to Vote." In *Lowering the Voting Age to 16: Learning from Real Experiences Worldwide*, 211–30. Palgrave Studies in Young People and Politics. Palgrave Macmillan, 2020.

17. Grabenstein, Hannah. "Should 16-Year-Olds Be Allowed to Vote?" *News Organization. PBS*, April 28, 2018. https://www.pbs.org/newshour/politics/should-16 -year-olds-be-allowed-to-vote

18. Perry, Douglas. "Oregon Lawmakers Seek to Lower Voting Age in State to 16, so Teens Can 'Protect Their Future.'" *News Organization. The Oregonian/ OregonLive*, February 19, 2019. https://www.oregonlive.com/politics/2019/02/o regon-lawmakers-seek-to-lower-voting-age-in-state-to-16-so-teens-can-protect-their -future.html

19. Kasperowicz, Pete. "House Rejects Democratic Push to Let 16-Year-Olds Vote." *Washington Examiner*, March 7, 2019. https://www.washingtonexaminer .com/news/house-rejects-democratic-push-to-let-16-year-olds-vote

20. Yang 2020. "Policy: Lower the Voting Age to 16." Political Campaign. Yang 2020, n.d. https://www.yang2020.com/policies/votingage/

21. Franklin, Mark N. *Voter Turnout and the Dynamics of Electoral Competition in Established Democracies since 1945*. New York, NY: Cambridge University Press, 2004.

22. Hart, Daniel, and Robert Atkins. "American Sixteen-and Seventeen-Year-Olds Are Ready to Vote." *ANNALS of the American Academy of Political and Social Science* 833, no. 1 (2011): 201–22. https://journals.sagepub.com/doi/10.1177/00027 16210382395

23. Hart, Daniel, and James Youniss. *Renewing Democracy in Young America*. New York, NY: Oxford University Press, 2017.

24. Zeglovits, Eva, and Julian Aichholzer. "Are People More Inclined to Vote at 16 than at 18? Evidence for the First-Time Voting Boost among 16-to 25-Year-Olds

in Austria." *Journal of Elections, Public Opinion and Parties* 24, no. 3 (2014): 351–63. https://www.tandfonline.com/doi/full/10.1080/17457289.2013.872652; and Zeglovits, Eva, and Martina Zandonella. "Political Interest of Adolescents before and after Lowering the Vote Age: The Case of Austria." *Journal of Youth Studies* 16, no. 8 (2013): 1084–104. https://www.tandfonline.com/doi/abs/10.1080/13676261.2013 .793785

25. Gallego, Aina. *Unequal Political Participation Worldwide.* New York, NY: Cambridge University Press, 2015.

26. Achen, Christopher, and Larry Bartels. "Democracy for Realists: Holding up a Mirror to the Electorate." *Juncture* 22, no. 4 (2016): 269–75. https://doi.org/10.1111 /j.2050-5876.2016.00873.x

27. Uggen, Christopher, Ryan Larson, and Sarah Shannon. "6 Million Lost Voters: State-Level Estimates of Felony Disenfranchisement, 2016." *The Sentencing Project*, October 6, 2016. https://www.sentencingproject.org/publications/6-million-lost-vot ers-state-level-estimates-felony-disenfranchisement-2016/

28. Vasilogambros, Matt. "Thousands Lose Right to Vote Under 'Incompetence' Laws." *News.* Stateline, March 21, 2018. https://www.pewtrusts.org/en/research-an d-analysis/blogs/stateline/2018/03/21/thousands-lose-right-to-vote-under-incompe tence-laws

29. Chan, Tak Wing, and Matthew Clayton. "Should the Voting Age Be Lowered to Sixteen? Normative and Empirical Considerations." *Political Studies* 54, no. 3 (2006): 533–58. https://journals.sagepub.com/doi/10.1111/j.1467-9248.2006.00620.x

30. Chan and Clayton. "Should the Voting Age Be Lowered to Sixteen?", 554.

31. Leininger, Arndt, and Thorsten Faas. "Votes at 16 in Germany: Examining Subnational Variation." In *Lowering the Voting Age to 16: Learning from Real Experiences Worldwide*, 143–66. Palgrave Studies in Young People and Politics. Palgrave Macmillan, 2020, 161.

32. Bergh, Johannes, and Jan Eichhorn. "Introduction." In *Lowering the Voting Age to 16: Learning from Real Experiences Worldwide*, 1–12. Palgrave Studies in Young People and Politics. Palgrave Macmillan, 2020.

33. Milner, Henry. "Political Knowledge, Civic Education and Voting at 16." In *Lowering the Voting Age to 16: Learning from Real Experiences Worldwide*, 65–79. Palgrave Studies in Young People and Politics. Palgrave Macmillan, 2020.

34. Eichhorn, Jan, and Johannes Bergh, eds. *Lowering the Voting Age to 16: Learning from Real Experiences Worldwide.* Palgrave Studies in Young People and Politics. Palgrave Macmillan, 2020.

35. Franklin. *Voter Turnout and the Dynamics of Electoral Competition.*

36. Franklin, Mark N. "Consequences of Lowering the Voting Age to 16: Lessons from Comparative Research." In *Lowering the Voting Age to 16: Learning from Real Experiences Worldwide*, 13–41. Palgrave Studies in Young People and Politics. Palgrave Macmillan, 2020.

37. Petraca. "Does Voting at a Younger Age Have an Effect on Satisfaction."

38. Khazan, Olga. "Argentina Lowers Its Voting Age to 16." *The Washington Post.* n.d., sec. WorldViews. https://www.washingtonpost.com/news/worldviews/wp/ 2012/11/01/argentina-voting-age/?utm_term=.28a39cb9ad08

39. Eichhorn, Jan, Anne Heyer, and Christine Huebner. "Who Influences the Formation of Political Attitudes and Decisions in Young People? Evidence from the Referendum on Scottish Independence." *D Part Think Tank for political participation*, April 2014, 13. https://pdfs.semanticscholar.org/db4a/cddd2257a15454396 0b79c672c03f47733b3.pdf

40. Huebner, Christine, and Jan Eichhorn. "Votes at 16 in Scotland: Political Experiences Beyond the Vote Itself." In *Lowering the Voting Age to 16: Learning from Real Experiences Worldwide*, 121–42. Palgrave Studies in Young People and Politics. Palgrave Macmillan, 2020.

41. Huebner and Eichhorn. "Votes at 16 in Scotland," 126–27.

42. Odegard, Guro, Johannes Bergh, and Jo Saglie. "Why Did Young Norwegians Mobilize: External Events or Early Enfranchisement?" In *Lowering the Voting Age to 16: Learning from Real Experiences Worldwide*, 189–210. Palgrave Studies in Young People and Politics. Palgrave Macmillan, 2020.

43. Douglas," Lowering the Voting Age from the Ground Up."

44. Douglas," Lowering the Voting Age from the Ground Up," 224.

45. Toots, Anu, and Tonu Idnurm. "Modernizing Voting in a Post-Transition Country: The Estonian Experience of Lowering the Voting Age." In *Lowering the Voting Age to 16: Learning from Real Experiences Worldwide*, 167–87. Palgrave Studies in Young People and Politics. Palgrave Macmillan, 2020, 182.

46. Zeglovits and Zandonella. "Political Interest of Adolescents," 1089.

47. Bergh, Johannes. "Does Voting Rights Affect the Political Maturity of 16-and 17-Year-Ols? Findings from the 2011 Norwegian Voting-Age Trial." *Electoral Studies* 32, no. 1 (2013): 90–100. https://www.sciencedirect.com/science/article/pii/ S0261379412001333?via percent3Dihub

48. Aichholzer, Julian, and Sylvia Kritzinger. "Voting at 16 in Practice; A Review of the Austrian Case." In *Lowering the Voting Age to 16: Learning from Real Experiences Worldwide*, 81–101. Palgrave Studies in Young People and Politics. Palgrave Macmillan, 2020.

49. Huebner and Eichhorn. "Votes at 16 in Scotland," 140.

50. Milner. "Political Knowledge, Civic Education and Voting at 16," 71.

51. Toots and Idnurm. "Modernizing Voting in a Post-Transition Country."

52. Aichholzer and Kritzinger. "Voting at 16 in Practice," 92.

53. Petraca. "Does Voting at a Younger Age Have an Effect on Satisfaction."

54. Hart and Atkins. "American Sixteen-and Seventeen-Year Olds," 214.

55. Zeglovits and Zandonella. "Political Interest of Adolescents."

56. Hart and Atkins. "American Sixteen-and Seventeen-Year-Olds."

57. Bhatti, Yosef, and Kasper M. Hansen. "Leaving the Nest and the Social Act of Voting: Turnout among First-Time Voters." *Journal of Elections, Public Opinion and Parties* 22, no. 4 (November 2012): 380–406. https://www.tandfonline.com/doi/ abs/10.1080/17457289.2012.721375

58. Zeglovits and Aichholzer. "Are People More Inclined to Vote at 16 than at 18?"

59. Larsen, Erik Gahner, Klaus Levinsen, and Ulrik Kjaer. "Democracy for the Youth? The Impact of Mock Elections on Voting Age Attitudes." *Journal of*

Elections, Public Opinion and Parties 26, no. 4 (2016): 435–51. https://www.tandfonl ine.com/doi/full/10.1080/17457289.2016.1186031

60. Leininger and Faas. "Votes at 16 in Germany," 163.

61. Eichhorn, Jan, and Johannes Bergh. "Conclusion." In *Lowering the Voting Age to 16: Learning from Real Experiences Worldwide*, 231–41. Palgrave Studies in Young People and Politics. Palgrave Macmillan, 2020, 238.

62. Wagner, Markus, David Johann, and Sylvia Kritzinger. "Voting at 16: Turnout and the Quality of Vote Choice." *Electoral Studies* 31, no. 2 (2012): 372–83. https ://www.sciencedirect.com/science/article/pii/S0261379412000212?via percent3Di-hub, 381.

63. Eichhorn, and Bergh. "Conclusion," 233.

64. Franklin. *Voter Turnout and the Dynamics of Electoral Competition.*

65. Zeglovits and Zandonella. "Political Interest of Adolescents," also Milner, Henry. *The Internet Generation: Engaged Citizens or Political Dropouts*. Lebanon, NH: Tufts University Press, 2010.

66. Jones, Stephen R. G. "Was There a Hawthorne Effect?" *American Journal of Sociology* 98, no. 3 (1992): 451–68. https://www.journals.uchicago.edu/doi/10.1086 /230046

Chapter 2

Voting, American Style

Chapter 1 established the proposition that 16–17-year-olds have the capacity to be competent voters and full citizens. Moving from the logical to the empirical we discovered that 16–17-year-old voters are not only comparable to the rest of the electorate. Evidence from Latin American and European elections confirmed the puzzling finding that if anything, 16–17-year-olds seem to be better citizens than their slightly older cohorts, at least in terms of voting behavior. But this is a low bar to clear. Just catching up to the next-to-last place team is rarely inspiring. After establishing the proposition that 16–17-year-olds voting would not presage the end of representative democracy, my attention was drawn to the intersection of this proposed reform with the larger problems afflicting contemporary democracy. The anomalous finding that 16–17-year-olds outperform 18–21-year-olds re-entered my thinking when the question of poor turnout by 18-year-olds came into focus.

In truth neither the student nor I thought that we would likely see this reform enacted in the United States. Our interest was drawn more to the intellectual challenge of understanding the curious features of voting in the United States. Thus far, Votes at 16 has only been enacted at a few local levels in the United States. However, the movement has gained traction, and there has been a dramatic switch in how this topic is addressed. Now, when I mention the book I am working on with the unlucky passenger who has the airplane seat next to mine, the response I generally get is that the idea sounds plausible. But, with all this good news to this point in the journey, it was naturally time to consider how this reform might interact with the bigger political picture.

The student and I worked together in an independent study course on this topic, and we kept finding new angles to the issue. We first reviewed the historical record of voting rights in the United States. We were prepared for an inspiring story, with heroic figures full of righteous determination fighting entrenched interests and overcoming tremendous odds, ultimately leading to success. But we soon discovered that resistance to, and removal of, voting rights also characterizes our voting history.[1]

Efforts to extend the franchise to new groups invariably face questions about the degree to which the new group would possess the requisite mental and emotional qualities appropriate to the responsibility of voting. We recognized that the prospective 16–17-year-olds age group also shares at least some characteristics of earlier out-groups that were originally considered ill-suited for the high level of political thought required for responsible voting. That 16-year-olds lack the interest and the knowledge to participate effectively mirrors claims made against earlier groups that have been added to the electorate over our history. We acknowledged that when the idea of extending the franchise to a new group is first broached the initial responses are typically overwhelmingly skeptical and/or openly hostile. And this is appropriate. Voting is an essential element of representative democracy and decisions about who can and who cannot vote should not be taken lightly.

Centuries ago, Christian theologians vigorously debated how many angels could dance on the head of a pin, but they never debated the existence of angels. Contemporary political philosophers debate whether there is a responsibility, duty, or obligation for eligible citizens to vote, but they never argue that if no one is allowed or chooses to vote the ensuing political system is legitimate. As expressed by Mayne and Geissel, "High-quality democracy cannot simply be understood in terms of the existence of particular kinds of democratic institutions, the most incontrovertible of which are free and fair elections: it is also defined by whether citizens actually turn out to vote in those elections."[2] What is subject to debate is who among the citizenry shall be allowed to vote. If the United States has moved toward "a more perfect union" since its founding it can be measured by the expansion of the electorate to include populations that were previously excluded from the franchise. Few would dispute that the expansion of the electorate by race, gender, and age, makes the United States more democratic. We could, however, argue about whether more democracy is better than less democracy. For example, is the Electoral College better than electing the president by national popular vote? In principle, I am on the side of those who believe that the cure for perceived ills of democracy is more democracy.[3]

Curiously, the US Constitution and its Bill of Rights is remarkably silent on the question of who can and cannot vote.[4] It reflects the historical reality that the states assembled at Philadelphia in 1787 were virtually independent countries. In fact, as Lichtman has documented, at our national founding it was universally recognized that representative democracy was the plan, but wide differences across the several states marked the eligible electorates.[5]

At the time, there was enough variation in voting rights throughout the states, that the founders feared that settling on any one set of guidelines would alienate one or more states and perhaps endanger the ratification of the proposed Constitution. The states had no interest in coming to an agreement on voting requirements, though they all accepted that the constitutional government required voting. The repercussions of this early and non-controversial decision are several and very important. Consequently, voting in the United States manifests itself in accordance with our decentralized federal political system.

A critically important aspect of the federal nature of elections in the United States is that states have wide latitude in determining who is eligible to vote. This has positive and negative impacts. This aspect of federalism has the advantage of allowing states to adjust their voting rules to compete for new residents—to grow the economy, and to gain greater representation in the House of Representatives. Among those groups that were allowed to vote in various states early in our history were African Americans and women. Some states did not restrict voting to citizens, but also allowed well-behaved foreigners who resided in the jurisdiction to vote. In some early cases, state actions took the form of loosening requirements and thereby expanding the electorate. A widely shared but quickly eliminated restriction was the property requirement. As Western territories sought to attract residents, they dangled the right to vote as an inducement. Some early elites appraised the unfolding Industrial Revolution and recognized that cities would grow and honorable men would soon make their livings separate from property ownership.

One underappreciated consequence of the federal voting system is how it renders states immune to the intuitive desire to have as many voters as possible. If the president, for example was elected by national popular vote, then each state would seek to maximize its citizens' votes, hoping to swing the national election in their direction. But, with the Electoral College, this need is superfluous. Each state's Electoral Vote is set by the number of senators (two per state) and House of Representatives members (based on population, not on voters). Thus, there is no advantage for a state to have a higher percentage of its citizens voting, which makes suppressing votes a viable option that can be pursued or resisted based on political calculations. Every party has an interest in keeping the demographic group that supports the rival party, from voting. In the last century, this played out with the Republican Party becoming a mainly White party while the Democratic Party became a mixed-race party. Consequently, under the federal-state voting system, the Republicans are structurally inclined toward seeking to repress the votes of non-White citizens, and to block some non-citizens from entering the country for fear of how they will eventually vote.[6]

On the negative side, federalism, by placing the voter at the mercy of the state legislature decisions regarding voting requirements, means that the states were free to exclude whatever groups they chose. Thus, states were free to tighten their voting restrictions in order to exclude unpopular groups from voting. At our founding, voting rights in all states had economic requirements. Elites originally could not accept that a non-property owner could have the interests of the entire polity at heart.[7] These were justified by equating economic resources with a stake in society's well-being. They believed that economic independence meant political independence, whereas those without economic resources would be subject to undue influence by those with money and prestige and would be subject to corruption by those who would seek to buy their vote directly or indirectly. This is comparable to the way that some critics of the 16-year-old vote claim that those youngsters will be dominated by their parents and/or their school teachers resulting in them not casting genuinely free votes.[8]

Except for the notable exception of expanding the electorate by abolishing the property requirement, the overwhelming early trend was toward tightening voting requirements culminating in a very restrictive electorate across virtually all states. For example, in 1800 only 5 of the 16 states prevented African Americans from voting, while in 1860, 28 of the 33 states prevented them from participating.[9] Thus, the adult White male resident citizen became essentially the only eligible voter in each of the states, even though states could define their voters as they choose. Even then there was still variance on what age makes an adult, and how long someone had to reside in the jurisdiction to become an eligible voter.

This less than inspiring flip side of the story of the ever-expanding electorate is vividly apparent in the story of the disenfranchisement of southern African Americans. When the 15th Amendment in 1870 extended the right to vote to African American men, the implementation was left in the hands of the southern state governments. After Reconstruction ended in 1877, the evolution of Jim Crow Laws, including but not limited to voting rights, was met with little resistance from the national government, as those laws were considered state jurisdictional matters (and a good idea by many national political elites).[10] In this sense the exclusion of southern African Americans from the electorate was a direct product of the Constitutional silence.

From our 21st-century vantage points, some of the restrictions might seem to us as reasonable (citizenship requirement) and others as blatantly and unfairly discriminatory (males only). This negative power to exclude groups from the electorate has been reduced by actions such as the 1964 Constitutional Amendment (24th) prohibiting Poll taxes, the 1965 Voting Rights Act that prohibited discrimination in voting rights based on race, as well as the Constitutional Amendments which have extended suffrage to African Americans (15th), women (19th), and citizens who are 18 or older (26th).

These restrictions on the negative power of states do not restrict their positive power to expand the electorate. As relates to this proposed reform, the Constitution leaves open the opportunity for individual states to adopt Votes at 16, without getting any sort of national legislation passed. In fact, a number of states made changes toward Votes at 18 decades before it was incorporated into federal law, before being adopted as the 26th Amendment.[11] Georgia pioneered this in 1943, in the midst of World War II.

When national trends reversed direction, and moved toward expanding the electorate, changes occurred episodically. Since the Civil War the franchise has been substantially expanded five times—to African Americans (1870), women (1920), Native Americans (1924); in the 1960s the Civil Rights Movement and federal legislation extended de facto voting rights to African Americans who had been de facto excluded from the franchise, and then to 18-year-olds (1971). Wars figured into each of these expansions of the suffrage, to varying degrees.[12] Two (15th and 26th Amendments) are very direct and cannot be understood outside the context of war, and the other three (19th Amendment, Indian Citizenship Act of 1924, Voting Rights Act of 1965) are less direct, but the connections are clear. A brief discussion of each of these follows.

The 15th Amendment, ratified in 1870, granted suffrage to African American men. This right was gained though public advocacy efforts of spokespersons such as Frederick Douglass, and of course because of the Civil War. Many believed that granting the right to vote to African American men was the final act of the Civil War and was justified by the important role African American troops played on the Union side.

Prior to passage of the 26th Amendment in 1971, a strong majority of 18–19-year-olds opposed getting the right to vote.[13] The reluctance of the beneficiaries was overcome with two lines of reasoning. One was the Vietnam War and its draft of 18-year-olds. If taxation without representation was tyranny, what could be said of drafting and sending people to the jungles of Southeast Asia without representation? Separate, but not unrelated, was the sense at the end of the 1960s that the American political system was in perilous condition and in danger of losing its legitimacy. Nightly news reports were filled with massive street protests in favor of civil rights and against the war in Vietnam; political assassinations; cities ablaze; university students occupying administration buildings; and two parties with "not a dime's worth of difference" in the words of firebrand George Wallace. In that context, the 18-year-old vote amendment was passed without it being demanded.[14] The adults hoped that the energy of young voters would infuse the system with enthusiasm and new positive ideas. And the youth of the 1960s/1970s were full of ideas, some of them good (Make Love Not War) and some not so good (Don't Trust Anyone Over 30).

The ratification of the 19th Amendment in 1920, occurred in the temporal shadow of World War I. The link between the two is less direct than the previous two examples, but the increased role of women in the wartime economy during World War I certainly bolstered the case that they could be competent voters. Prior to this, men had categorized the work of women in managing a household and nurturing a family as fundamentally different from, and inferior to, the work men were doing in the marketplace, the corridors of government, and the battlefields.

The Indian Citizenship Act of 1924 perhaps represents the weakest direct connection to war. Passage did not follow the end of any specific war, but its connection is visible through the earlier wars in the American west. In truth, most of US governmental history with Native Americans is connected to warfare.

Arguably, the greatest positive political activity in the United States in my lifetime was the passage and implementation of the Voting Rights Act of 1965 and associated civil rights legislation that were passed around the same time. And the connection between President Johnson's civil rights domestic programs and the War in Vietnam are clearly evident.[15] Controversial heavyweight boxing champion Muhammad Ali phrased it this way in 1967: "Why should they ask me to put on a uniform and go 10,000 miles from home and drop bombs and bullets on Brown people in Vietnam while so-called Negro people in Louisville are treated like dogs and denied simple human rights?"[16] It is instructive that Ali's quote comes two years after passage of the landmark Voting Rights Act, indicating that political equality does not automatically follow legislative actions. As historian Carol Anderson documented, US history is replete with efforts to deny "eligible" voters from casting votes, and these efforts are with us still.[17]

The relationship between war and extension of suffrage is relevant to the topic of extending the vote to 16–17-year-olds because it is becoming common to hear of schools as war zones.[18] This may sound far-fetched to many, but these arguments are structured similarly to those at the time of the 18-year-old voting amendment. Arguments were made in both cases that when lives are at stake those at risk should have a vote in matters pertaining to their well-being—the Vietnam War in one case and gun control laws in the other case. Elected politicians could (and eventually did) end the Vietnam War and they can (and might someday) enact strong laws regulating guns.

Although the student I had worked with eventually graduated leaving me on my own, this idea continued simmering in my thinking. As a little-j justice issue, the question did not come to a full boil until I placed the issue in a comparative democratic context. Realizing that the issue of youth voting was related to concerns about dropping voting rates across the democratic world raised the stakes of this reform. What impact, if any, would lowering the voting age have on the overall turnout rates? The early indications were not promising. When voting rates are displayed by age cohort, the results form a straight line downward. The oldest cohorts have the highest voting rates and each younger cohort votes at lower rates, ultimately landing with the youngest cohorts having the lowest of all. Thus, adding even younger groups to the electorate looks to many like a recipe for even greater decline.

As I continued my consideration of this reform, it was not long before I confronted considerable angst and disdain among scholars and pundits. Angst was focused on the declining voting rates across the established democratic world. Disdain was focused on the young generations who were in last place in the voting turnout ratings. This is important because Votes at 16 is being advanced at a time where questions abound about the legitimacy of democracy.

It was distressingly easy to find concerns about the political status of Western liberal democracies including, but not limited to, the United States. If anything, the voices of concern have grown louder as the years have passed. Several recent works have drawn attention to the existential threat facing liberal democracy while reminding us that the persistence of liberal democracy is not foreordained.[19] Books written by serious scholars with titles like *It's Even Worse Than it Looks* (2012) and *How Democracies Die* (2018) capture the flavor[20]. Contemporary liberal democracy is on the defensive with many critics and ordinary citizens deciding that either the system is fatally flawed or that our conception of how politics really works is fundamentally erroneous.

Achen and Bartels summarized the findings of generations of political scientists and reached a couple of dispiriting conclusions. One is that most voters are unknowledgeable about the issues, candidates, and parties.[21] The other is that elections are virtually random in terms of being connected to the performance of governments. Amy Chua (2018) suggests that focusing on individually rational citizens is mistaken because we are tribal in nature.[22] More recent concerns have shifted away from absent voters to the rise of anti-system voters. Legitimacy of democratic governments seems to be at stake since non-voters are "voting" against the democratic political system. Anti-system voters can come from the left or the right sides of the political spectrum but currently those of greatest concern are emerging on the right, sometimes far right, portion of the spectrum. In previous decades, the preponderant number of anti-system votes were cast from the left side.

Elections are routinely followed with challenges and claims of voter suppression (when Democrats lose) or voter fraud (when Republicans lose). Gerrymandering is reaching epic proportions if the cable news reports are to be believed. Certainly, the American electoral system does not translate votes directly into victories. Since 2000, the Electoral College has twice (2000, 2016) awarded the Presidency to the candidate who finished second in the popular vote, making it a constitutionally generated outcome. At the state level, studies have documented how the political party that receives the most votes often wins fewer House seats than the second-place party.[23]

Survey research conducted recently supports these worrying signs. At the onset of the Trump Administration in 2017, several scholars established Bright Line Watch and employed YouGov to conduct online surveys of American experts (935 Political Science faculty) and general public (2,000 citizens). They sought to provide running evaluations of how these groups view the quality of American democracy during the Trump Presidency.[24] In their seventh iteration of their report covering October/November 2018, they identified three topics (out of 27) in which the public has seen significant deterioration with numbers dropping significantly:

1) Law enforcement investigations of public officials or their associates are free from political influence or interference;
2) Government officials are legally sanctioned for misconduct;
3) Government officials do not use public office for private gain.

These concerns are both directly connected with President Donald Trump, and speak to the legitimacy of the entire political system. The focus of these items is on the accountability of government officials. The trends become more vivid when broken down by Trump supporters vs. non-Trump supporters. Large gaps emerged on a number of topics with the following questions having a gap of more than 20 points: Some of these concerns focus on accountability—others on fairness of representations, voting, and elections.

1) All citizens have equal opportunity to vote;
2) Elections are free from foreign influence;
3) The geographic boundaries of electoral districts do not systematically advantage any particular political party;
4) All adult citizens enjoy the same legal and political rights;
5) All votes have equal impact on election outcomes;
6) The legislature is able to effectively limit executive power;
7) Executive authority cannot be expanded beyond constitutional limits.

The Pew Research Center found similar rising concerns about the health and legitimacy of the American political system.[25] Using a large pool of Americans, they found that a majority believe that President Trump has "not too much respect" or "no respect" for America's democratic institutions. The question of whether they, the voters, are knowledgeable about politics and current issues generated a 56 percent response rate of no or little confidence in the political wisdom of the American people. Pew also found a strong partisan divide with Republicans (party in power) more optimistic about the status of democracy than are Democrats (party out of power). That there is a divide is not necessarily significant but the depth of the divide is worrisome.

Both these reports indicate a dissatisfaction with the way government works (sometimes focusing on structural factors such as gerrymandered Congressional districts) as well as on norms (such as the positive value of compromising in politics, and agreeing on basic facts) around which American politics has traditionally operated.[26] It is worth noting that the erosion of norms was documented well before the 2016 election of Donald Trump. It is commonly heard that the deep partisan divide traces back to the political struggles of the 1990s between President Bill Clinton and House Speaker Newt Gingrich. A vivid example from June 2018 showed that Republicans preferred North Korean dictator Kim Jong Un over the former and soon to be again Speaker of the House of Representatives, Nancy Pelosi.[27] As Levitsky and Ziblatt pointed out, one of four earmarks of authoritarian behavior is "Denial of the legitimacy of political opponents."[28]

Political observers have long been sounding the alarm about disturbing trends in the American political system. Although many dimensions of the democratic problem have been addressed, much of the early focus was on declining voting rates across the democratic world. This trend was also noted with concern in the European democracies. However, since European voting rates are significantly higher than in the United States the concerns there were not as profound.[29]

It is conceivable that declining voting rates are a symptom of voter satisfaction and complacency, that the non-voters think everything is working well. Senate Majority Mitch McConnell (R-Ky) opined that "relatively low voter turnout is a sign of a relatively content democracy."[30] Conceivable, but not likely. Folk wisdom suggests that the decline in voting is correlated with the decline in trust for democratic regimes. A healthy democracy requires high citizen participation. Oftentimes, the lack of political knowledge is portrayed as a harbinger of political crises. If people lack knowledge and abstain from voting then the future of the democratic system is at risk, or so it is commonly said. We are now confronting an electorate that is awakening although still low on political knowledge. The impressive mid-term turnout in the 2018 elections was generally portrayed as a sign of political crisis, rather than as a hopeful sign of engaged citizens. The turnout was only high, it is argued, because the highly polarized political landscape was fraught with peril.[31]

Two characteristics of Western democratic societies are trending in a direction that is correlated with high voting rates. The first characteristic is the aging population. Voting cohorts increase their voting rates as they age. This seems to hold until an advanced age at which point the elderly turnout rates begin to decline. It is noteworthy that the age where decline begins is rising, because of advances in the cognitive and physical abilities of elderly people. The second characteristic is the rising educational levels of democratic citizens. As Gallego documented extensively across the democratic world, with very few exceptions, those with higher educational attainment vote at higher rates than those with less education. So, as democracies rise in educational attainment, and in age, they should be voting at higher rates, but that is not the case when we look at country-wide voting data. Instead, the voting rates have been trending downward.

... AND YOUTH ARE TO BLAME

Naturally, my attention shifted to the reasons for the dismal turnout of young voters. The older citizens are significantly more likely to vote than are the younger citizens. We can look at this issue either due to the characteristics of the youth, or due to the circumstances facing the youth as they become eligible voters. Recent cohorts have entered the age of majority with declining voting rates, declining economic growth rates, and rapidly proliferating non-political entertainment options. Scholars have long debated the specific characteristics of political generations.[32] We shall not attempt to adjudicate those disputes here. But we can discuss certain trends that carry across recent generations.[33]

Three merit attention and they are found in very different places within society. One is found within the younger generations, the second is found

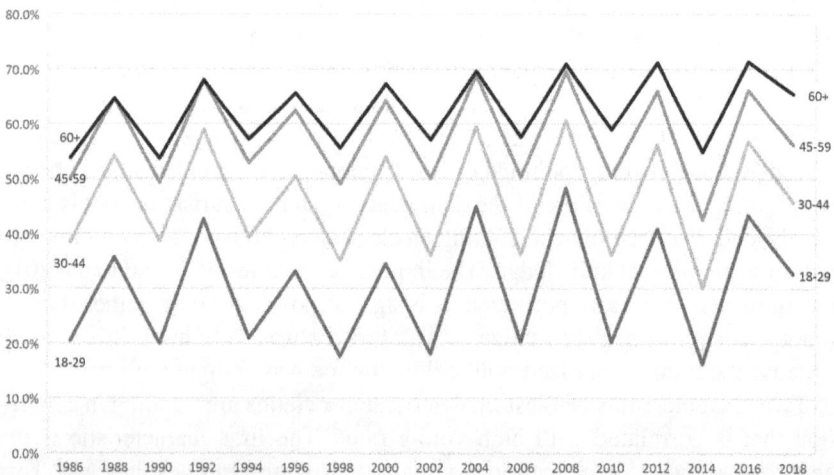

Figure 2.1 Turnout by Age. Source: United States Election Project Voter Turnout Demographics.

in the circumstances in which young generations have found themselves, and the third puts a finer point on that with its emphasis on social media. Beginning with the first, scholars have debated whether the evidence of declining allegiance to liberal democracy is the fault of young people or not. These explanations locate the problem with individuals failing to fulfill their democratic obligations. These tend to pay particular attention to the younger generations who are said to be shirking their duties.

The second explanation locates the problems in the external environment that young voters inhabit. These problems are identified as globalization, and the general inability of liberal democratic governments to make effective decisions. Some place the blame on national governments that are unable to deliver satisfactory outcomes and seem feckless or powerless in the face of globalization. Some see the blame resting within national political borders as in the gerrymandering situations described as representatives selecting their voters rather than voters selecting their representatives.

The third explanation claims that social media is a quintessential global phenomenon that individuals interact with in their own unique ways.[34] It spares humans from their criticisms and blames technology—specifically the internet, telephones, and social media in all its proliferating forms. These are said to rob humans of the ability to remain focused on important political matters. Neither of these affect young people only, and certainly youth are not responsible for causing either trend. It is probably more accurate to think of young adults being the victims, in the sense that both trends are shaping their lives with or without their consent.

These competing explanations came into focus for me when I adopted Martin Wattenberg's text *Is Voting for Young People?* in a subsequent iteration of the Introduction to Political Science course.[35] The book opened my eyes to a powerful critique of youth voting that seemed to undermine the idea of 16-year-old voting. Wattenberg amassed several sets of data depicting the sad status of contemporary youth as political animals.[36] First, among currently eligible citizens, younger citizens in the United States and other Western democracies vote at lower rates than older citizens. This has been happening over several decades and the trend does not seem to be ending. More importantly, low-voting youth will increase their voting rates over time, but they will not attain the same rates of voting as their elder generations. Wattenberg is very clear that he does not see low youth turnout to be a natural stage in a citizen's life.[37] The life-cycle theory asserts that as citizens go through life their likelihood of voting naturally increases. The natural aspect comes from learning more about the political world and recognizing the impact that elected officials have on taxing and spending issues. Gallego agrees that the low turnout youth are a generational and not just a life-cycle problem. Generations born after 1950 have been voting at lower rates than life-cycle would have predicted.[38] Second, younger voters have less political knowledge than older voters. The theorists claim therefore, that adding even younger voters will decrease the overall voter turnout rates and exacerbate the sense that the political system is losing legitimacy.

My students, who as political science majors were probably already registered to vote, chafed at Wattenberg's depiction of their generation's political apathy and ignorance. They strenuously claimed that they simply get their information from other news sources, not the newspapers or television newscasts that Wattenberg loves, and that they frequently became engaged politically in ways other than voting. They described their wide variety of news sources, and the many politically oriented groups in which they participate. Not surprisingly, most of the things they mentioned were completely alien to me.

Unlike other scholars, Wattenberg does not claim that any particular aspect of US elections is at fault for these declines. The two most prominent criticisms focus on the way American elections are held. Specifically, the Tuesday election tradition, and the difficulty of registering to vote. Wattenberg showed that prior to the 1970s young and older voters turned out at nearly the same rates. In his view, we did not have to do too much to get youth to vote back then, but now no matter what we do, youth today tend to vote at very low levels. He also noted that drops in participation rates have been seen across the democratic world despite how different those electoral and party systems are from each other. Thus, he lays the blame on the proliferation and fragmentation of the news media and entertainment more broadly. Over the last few decades the news media has become decentralized, and news must compete with 24-hour sports networks and movies on demand, for the attention of all citizens.[39] Older citizens have developed habits of news consumption that lead to regular voting behaviors. Younger citizens have not developed those news consumption patterns, instead getting news from a variety of sources. But, Wattenberg notes, their command of political news and knowledge is very low because youth consume many other things on their electronic devices and relatively little news. In sum, Wattenberg makes a compelling case that youth in America and other Western democracies are less knowledgeable and less interested in politics than previous generations.[40]

Other scholars have entered the fray, introducing concepts such as deconsolidation to refer to the decline in the population's adherence to and embrace of democratic values. Foa and Mounk argued that survey evidence shows young people do not have the same appreciation of democratic tenets as older generations.[41] They contended that the problem is much deeper than low voting rates. It goes to a loss in faith in the inherent goodness and utility of our political norms and institutions. Consequently, the strength of liberal democracy is ebbing as the youth become a larger part of the electorate.

Norris rejected this and contended that the survey data reveals a life-cycle phenomenon and not a chronic shift.[42] She also noted that where the populist outsiders generate election-winning strength, they get much more support from the older voters. She noted that the Brexit vote in the United Kingdom in summer 2016 coupled with Donald Trump's surprise victory in fall 2016 are exemplars of opposition to the prevailing system. In both cases the oldest generations voted for those outcomes the most and the youngest generations supported them the least.

An important work in the literature decrying the political apathy of young people is *Running from Office: Why Young Americans Are Turned Off to Politics*.[43] Its main argument is that in comparison to earlier generations the current one demonstrates very low interest in ever running for office. The authors found that only 11 percent of young people would even consider running for office, and that in the rare cases when their families discuss politics it is often unpleasant. Furthermore, their interactions with their peers tend to avoid politics due to its unappealing nature. Finally, they found that while students valued leadership qualities and roles, they did not associate those with politics. In other words, these young people are not apathetic; rather they maintain the traditional youthful desire to improve the world, it is just that they do not see politics as the avenue to follow.

Some of the reasons for these numbers are clear. Politics seems infused with a degree of nastiness that turns idealistic young people away. Political pundits are more intent on generating heat than light, to maximize viewers or clicks. Moreover, the nastiness rarely seems to implement effective solutions to pressing national problems, thereby generating an outlook that expects future generations to earn less than the current one.[44] It is worth noting that their research took place during the Obama Presidency whose 2008 election was a high-water mark for recent youthful political enthusiasm. So, we would expect that Obama would have inspired a youthful generation like the way John Kennedy did. But the record is mixed.

Although they show how young people are eschewing running for elective office, their evidence also shows that education coupled with participation can generate political interest and habits. The authors compared the 11 percent who were open to running for office with the 89 percent who were not, and found some interesting patterns. Among their findings was the correlation with taking a political science or government class in school and interest in running for office. Of the 11 percent, 60 percent had taken such a course, and among the 89 percent only 44 percent had.[45] This gap is surprising since all states have some sort of civics requirements, though some can be satisfied without passing a government, politics, or civics course.[46]

However, this essentially negative take on the political interest of this generation also holds out a sliver of hope that we can build upon. *Running from Office* discovers that even if students think politics is ugly and nasty, when they learn how politics works, they actually get interested in becoming involved. By comparison, those who think politics is bad and do not know much about the political system tend to be uninterested in getting politically involved. This is one of the strongest statements on how education can provide the nourishment for a new generation of engaged citizens. However, we are not doing this very well. In the words of the authors, "Those who tune in are far less likely to be turned off. The key to generating more political ambition among today's young people, then, seems to be hooking them on electoral politics and maintaining their interest, despite the unappealing nature of much of what they'll see."[47] Thus, despite their sincere concerns about the long-term effects of nasty partisan politics driving young people away from politics and weakening the public support for American democracy upon which the legitimacy of the system rests, they find already in place the mechanisms for rejuvenating the political system—Education! Especially, I might add, political science education.

Against this tide of pessimism stand a cohort of scholars led by Russell Dalton who side with my students when they rebelled against Wattenberg's indictment of them. They maintain that young people are participating in politics at a high and increasing level.[48] They reasonably define political participation broadly to include political acts beyond voting and thereby reduce the importance of voting in painting their overall pictures. Thus, the declining voting rates are only half of the picture. When other forms of political participation are measured including attending rallies, organizing protests, providing aid to those in need, etc. American youth outshine earlier generations.

Liberal democratic political systems allow and often encourage forms of political participation beyond voting. In the United States the First Amendment's protection of the freedom of speech was specifically designed to protect unpopular political speech. This opened the space for citizens to petition government and to protest political actions of which they disagree. Without those opportunities to express their political views, a political system characterized by elections is less than a liberal democracy.

Different forms of political participation vary in terms of how easy it is for the humblest citizens to partake. It is often noted that voting is the easiest form of political participation.[49] Other forms of political participation are even more skewed toward the richest and most educated citizens. As noted with the Global Citizen example, becoming active in an online forum seems infinitely easier and non-complicated in comparison to the red tape and deadlines that surround voting in the United States. But if we maintain our focus on voting, then ostensibly every adult citizen who is not incarcerated or a convicted felon or been deemed by a court to be mentally deficient, can vote.

Dalton divides attitudes toward political participation into two categories. One is the norm of duty-based citizenship and the other is the norm of engaged citizenship.[50] Voting is the quintessential type of duty-based citizenship. Helping prepare meals at a homeless shelter represents a standard type of engaged citizenship. Rather than worry about the fate of American democracy because young people are less interested in voting and running for political office, rejoice in the energy and imagination of the internet generation's ability to fashion new solutions to today's pressing problems. In a sense, they are taking seriously the feminist argument that the personal is political. Thus, the choices one makes in their eating, shopping, and online activities comprise the essence of living a political life. It is self-directed and stands in juxtaposition with the old-fashioned model where political apprentices work on election campaigns and work their way through the party apparatus to become candidates themselves—candidates who must satisfy this or that constituency group, must curry favor with this or that major financial donor, and slavishly follow strategies designed by their professional campaign manager.

Even if we accept Dalton's dichotomy, there is no reason that citizens cannot exhibit both archetypical types of citizenship. As a society, we should seek to produce complete citizens, and the good news is that there are few barriers that should keep engaged citizens from acquiring the habit of voting. When engaged citizens fail to vote they not only change the outcome of elections but also develop habits of not voting. So, the key is to get young people into the habit of voting while their reformist passions are still strong. We risk skewing future elections toward those who embody duty-based citizenship if we allow those who have or continue to embrace engaged citizenship to avoid voting. Engaged citizens whose engagement energies decrease over time will automatically be eligible to become duty-based citizens, but without having developed the habit of voting they will as a group, vote at lower rates than the duty-based citizens.

But the task of convincing engaged citizens to take up voting will not be easy. These advocates maintain that while they are not voting they are actively participating in ways that they find more meaningful for their generation. These youth see voting in a representative democracy as a poor substitution for real political action. This is not an irrational perspective. Anthony Downs illustrated the essential irrationality of voting if voting costs the citizen anything (time, energy, stress).[51] The chance that any one citizen's vote decides an election is miniscule. And the notion that a middle-aged (or older) White (usually) male (usually) will in any real sense "represent" the interest of today's youth seems quaint. It seems preposterous to wait two, or four, or six years for an opportunity to replace the elected politician. By contrast, volunteering at the food pantry, or joining a boycott against a badly behaving corporation, or signing petitions organized and distributed online, seems like real actions that can have more direct impacts. I can act as one of Dalton's duty-based citizens and try to convince the leaders of all the countries in the world to contribute resources toward ending global poverty in my lifetime, and failing that I can work to elect leaders who will promise to end poverty. Or, I can act as one of Dalton's engaged citizens and I can throw my energy and resources behind Global Citizen's effort to end global poverty.[52] Global Citizen will magnify my voice because their views on this issue align perfectly with mine. If they do not align perfectly, I will find another organization/website that does. Compare this with the desultory choices the two parties regularly put forward to voters. Even if the parties put forward charismatic candidates, the parties they represent are normally multi-issue entities, whereas I might only feel passionate about a particular issue.

Henry Milner's concern is youth who do not get politically socialized into the standard electoral processes. He chides the views championed by Dalton by saying that the old slogan "think globally act locally," has morphed into "bypass government, act individually."[53] To be fair, as a society we should also be interested in making duty-based citizens more engaged. However, that is left to Dalton and others to figure out. The focus here is on voting since that is the predicate upon which democracy rests. Without the accountability that elections provide, democracy weakens and when that accountability is skewed by unequal participation then the democracy itself is skewed.

Your political science professor will advise you, rightly, that pursuing both paths is possible. But, in a world where we must make choices, choosing to pursue the Global Citizen path is not irrational. Wattenberg devotes a chapter of his book to throwing water on this line of analysis by showing that today's youth do not volunteer more than older generations, and that much of what is measured are efforts by young people to pad their applications for college or for employment purposes.[54]

CONCLUSION

This chapter portrayed the evolution of voting rights in the United States as a long-standing political battleground. The direction of the historical arrow of voting rights in the past 100 years has been unmistakably pointing in the direction of expanding the electorate. The percentage of the American population that is eligible to register and vote has more than doubled since the 19th Amendment was passed. Nevertheless, the battle is not over. The numbers of incarcerated convicted felons who are ineligible to join the voting lists have climbed dramatically in the last few decades. Efforts to make voting more difficult, in the name of reducing voting fraud, continue apace. Beyond these cautionary cases, Votes at 16 is on the horizon.

In confronting the problem with youth political participation, we noted that there is more than one way to participate politically, but we insisted that voting should remain among the most universal manners of participation. We noted that one could be, and should strive to be, both a duty-based citizen who is a registered voter who follows elections closely, and an engaged citizen who is not restricted to only electoral politics.

With the arguments in favor of lowering the voting age and the evidence gathered thus far indicating that the worst dangers are overblown, all signs for Votes at 16 were pointing favorably. However, the question of how this change might interact with other voting trends lingered. This led to the realization that this issue was embedded in two different but not unrelated areas of concern within the voting landscape. We have just discussed the first area of concern, the low and declining voting rates within the United States and other Western democracies. Now it is time to discuss the second area of concern, the inequalities in voting behavior that are well known but often overlooked by scholars.

NOTES

1. Anderson, Carol. *One Person, No Vote: How Voter Suppression Is Destroying Our Democracy.* New York, NY: Bloomsbury Publishing, 2018.

2. Mayne, Quinton, and Brigitte Geissel. "Don't Good Democracies Need 'Good' Citizens? Citizen Dispositions and the Study of Democratic Quality." *Politics and Governance* 6, no. 1 (March 2018): 33–47. https://www.cogitatiopress.com/politicsandgovernance/article/view/1216

3. Achen, Christopher, and Larry Bartels. *Democracy for Realists: Why Elections Do Not Produce Responsive Government*, 52–89. Princeton, NJ: Princeton University Press, 2016, ch. 3.

4. Lichtman, Allan. *The Embattled Vote in America: From the Founding to the Present.* Cambridge, MA: Harvard University Press, 2018.

5. Lichtman. *The Embattled Vote in America*, 16.

6. Lichtman. *The Embattled Vote in America*, ch. 6, 147–79.

7. Lichtman. *The Embattled Vote in America*, 14–18.

8. Russell, Andrew. "The Case for Lowering the Voting Age Is Less Persuasive Now than at Any Point in the Last 50 Years." Political. *Democraticaudit.com*, May 16, 2014. https://www.democraticaudit.com/2014/05/16/highlighting-the-minimal-rights-accrued-by-16-year-olds-is-a-flawed-argument-for-lowering-the-voting-age/

9. Lichtman. *The Embattled Vote in America*, 37.

10. Woodward, C. Vann. *The Strange Career of Jim Crow.* 3rd ed. Oxford, UK: Oxford University Press, 1974.

11. Douglas, Joshua A. "Lowering the Voting Age from the Ground Up: The United States' Experience in Allowing 16-Year-Olds to Vote." In *Lowering the*

Voting Age to 16: Learning from Real Experiences Worldwide, 211–30. Palgrave Studies in Young People and Politics. Palgrave Macmillan, 2020.

12. Cultice, Wendell W. *Youth's Battle for the Ballot: A History of Voting Age in America*, 1–18. Contributions in Political Science 291. Westport, CT: Greenwood Press, 1992, ch.1.

13. Erskine, Hazel. "The Polls: The Politics of Age." *Public Opinion Quarterly* 35, no. 3 (1971): 482–95.

14. Beck, Paul Allen, and M. Kent Jennings. "Lowering the Voting Age: The Case of the Reluctant Electorate." *Public Opinion Quarterly* 33, no. 3 (1969): 370–79. https://academic.oup.com/poq/article-abstract/33/3/370/1830884?redirectedFrom=fulltext; and Erskine. "The Polls: The Politics."

15. Woods, Randall B. "The Politics of Idealism: Lyndon Johnson, Civil Rights, and Vietnam." *Diplomatic History* 31, no. 1 (December 11, 2006): 1–18. https://academic.oup.com/dh/article/31/1/1/356070

16. Orkand, Bob. "I Ain't Got No Quarrel With Them Vietcong." *New York Times*, June 27, 2017, sec. Opinion. https://www.nytimes.com/2017/06/27/opinion/muhammad-ali-vietnam-war.html

17. Anderson. *One Person, No Vote*, ch. 1, 1–43.

18. The Editors. "A School Is Not a Military Post." *Scientific American*, January 2018. https://www.scientificamerican.com/article/a-call-to-make-schools-safe-zones-not-war-zones/

19. Sunstein, Cass, ed. *Can It Happen Here? Authoritarianism in America*. New York, NY: Dey St., 2018; and "The Death of Democracy: Hitler's Rise to Power and the Downfall of the Weimar Republic." *New York Times Book Review*, June 17, 2018. https://search.proquest.com/docview/2060918535/fulltext/EBEACEBDF6C04638PQ/2?accountid=14968

20. Mann, Thomas E., and Norman J. Ornstein. *It's Even Worse That It Looks: How the American Constitutional System Collided with the New Politics of Extremism*. New York, NY: Basic Books, 2012; and Levitsky, Steven, and Daniel Ziblatt. *How Democracies Die*. New York, NY: Crown Publishing Group, 2018.

21. Achen and Bartels. *Democracy for Realists*, 36–41.

22. Chua, Amy. *Political Tribes: Group Instinct and the Fate of Nations*. New York, NY: Penguin Press, 2018.

23. Tamas, Bernard. "American Disproportionality: A Historical Analysis of Partisan Bias in Elections to the U.S. House of Representatives." *Election Law Journal* 18, no. 1 (2019): 47–62. https://www.liebertpub.com/doi/10.1089/elj.2017.0464

24. Bright Line Watch. "Bright Line Watch -- Wave 7 Report." Political Survey. Bright Line Watch, Oct/Nov2018. http://brightlinewatch.org/wave7/

25. Pew Research Center. "The Public, the Political System and American Democracy." *Polling Organization. Pew Research Center*, April 28, 2018. https://www.people-press.org/2018/04/26/the-public-the-political-system-and-american-democracy/

26. Bright Line Watch. "Bright Line Watch -- Wave 7 Report."

27. Shelbourne, Mallory. "Poll: Kim Jong Un Has Higher Approval among Republicans than Pelosi." *The Hill*, June 18, 2018. https://thehill.com/homenews/house/392756-poll-kim-jong-un-has-higher-approval-among-republicans-than-pelosi

28. Levitsky and Ziblatt. *How Democracies Die.*

29. Desilver, Drew. "U.S. Trails Most Developed Countries in Voter Turnout." *Polling Organization. Pew Research Center*, May 15, 2017. https://static1.squa respace.com/static/58706fbb29687f06dd219990/t/5b108a8d70a6ad1221aa63c1/1527 810701921/U.S+voter+turnout+lower+than+most+countries+-+Pew+May+2017.pdf

30. Lichtman. *The Embattled Vote in America*, 177.

31. Rojanasakul, Mira, Jeremy C. F. Lin, Lauren Leatherby, Alison McCartney, Demetrios Pogkas, and David Ingold. "Americans Actually Voted in the 2018 Midterms." *Bloomberg*, December 20, 2018. https://www.bloomberg.com/graphics/ 2018-midterm-election-turnout-shifts/

32. Milkman, Ruth. "A New Political Generation: Millennials and the Post-2008 Wave of Protest." *American Sociological Review* 82, no. 1 (2017): 1–31. https://jo urnals.sagepub.com/doi/10.1177/0003122416681031

33. McDonald, Michael P. "United States Election Project: Voter Turnout Demographics." *Political Data. United States Election Project.* Accessed March 7, 2020. http://www.electproject.org/home/voter-turnout/demographics

34. Milner. *The Internet Generation.*

35. Wattenberg, Martin. *Is Voting for Young People?* 4th ed. New York, NY: Routledge, 2016.

36. Wattenberg. I*s Voting for Young People?* ch. 5, 119–30.

37. Wattenberg. *Is Voting for Young People?* ch. 6, 131–50.

38. Gallego, Aina. "Where Else Does Turnout Decline Come from? Education, Age, Generation and Period Effects in Three European Countries." *Scandinavian Political Studies* 32, no. 1 (January 2009): 23–44. https://onlinelibrary.wiley.com/doi /full/10.1111/j.1467-9477.2008.00212.x

39. Milner. *The Internet Generation*, ch. 3, 53–76.

40. Wattenberg. I*s Voting for Young People?* ch. 3, 57–88.

41. Foa, Roberto Stefan, and Yascha Mounk. "The Signs of Deconsolidation." *Journal of Democracy* 28, no. 1 (January 2017): 5–16. https://www.journalofdemo cracy.org/articles/the-signs-of-deconsolidation/

42. Norris, Pippa. "Is Western Democracy Backsliding? Diagnosing the Risks." *Journal of Democracy*, no. April 2017, n.d. https://www.journalofdemocracy.org/wp -content/uploads/2018/12/Journal-of-Democracy-Web-Exchange-Norris_0.pdf

43. Lawless, Jennifer L., and Richard L. Fox. *Running from Office: Why Young Americans Are Turned off to Politics.* New York, NY: Oxford University Press, 2015.

44. Popken, Ben. "Only 37 Percent of Americans Think Their Kids Will Be Better Off." News. NBC News, June 6, 2017. https://www.nbcnews.com/business/consume r/only-37-percent-americans-think-their-kids-will-be-better-n768706

45. Lawless and Fox. *Running From Office*, 162

46. Center for Information & Research on Civic Learning and Engagement. "High School Civics Requirements and Assessments Vary Across the U.S." *Educational. Blog*, June 4, 2014. https://www.ecs.org/citizenship-education-policies/

47. Lawless and Fox. *Running From Office*, 143

48. Dalton, Russel J. *The Good Citizen: How a Younger Generation is Reshaping American Politics.* 2nd ed. Thousand Oaks, CA: CQ Press, 2015.

49. Dalton. *The Participation Gap.*

50. Dalton. *The Participation Gap.*

51. Achen. *Democracy for Realists*, 24.

52. "Global Citizen." Public Interest Organization, n.d. https://www.globalcitizen
.org/en/

53. Milner. *The Internet Generation,* 5.

54. Wattenberg. *Is Voting for Young People?*, ch. 7.

Chapter 3

Helping the Heavenly
Chorus Sound Better

Chapter 2 surveyed the political history of voting in the United States before turning to a discussion of youth voting behavior, as well as new forms of political participation. Now we place this issue into what a famous political scientist in 1997 called "Democracy's Unresolved Dilemma."[1] Like many things in the political world, voting may be an individual decision, but aggregate group patterns showing the uneven distribution of voting (and non-voting) emerge when we look at the typical demographic categories beloved by social scientists. While overall voting rates have declined across the board, this has not eliminated the inequalities that persist within electorates. We know that certain inequalities do, and always will exist in voting rates. Some citizens will vote and others will not. This is completely natural, but we suspect that the likelihood of voting is not randomly distributed throughout society. We also suspect that there might be a correlation of voting rates with the way the rules of voting evolved historically.

Political inequality is not a new or particularly unique American issue. Except for the few democracies that have compulsory voting, virtually all democratic states have certain citizen categories voting at higher rates than others. Since most compulsory voting countries have very light or nonex-istent enforcement, even they have inequality of voting rates.[2] Of course, countries with higher overall rates of voting will have less variation in voting across demographic groups.[3] Countries with 90 percent+ voting rates overall will typically have all major demographic categories at very high rates as well. When overall voting rates are much lower, as in the United States, there tend to be much wider gaps between the high and low demographic groups.

That there may be variation in voting rates is not necessarily problematic. Some variations might be good after all. As some old folks say, "Variety is the spice of life." But, when we use the term inequality instead of variation, we are typically assigning a negative value to it. Following from that is the belief that we should probably try to do something to reduce or eliminate that inequality. There are some who claim there is little difference between voters and non-voters on major political issues.[4] This seems improbable. Even if differences are slight, the absence of one set of non-voting voices will have repercussions that will accrue to the benefit of the voting group.

In this chapter, we explore the variation/inequality in voting behaviors within the American electorate. This is relevant to us because we want to understand what is required for us to fix low voting rates in the United States. Spoiler Alert: Votes at 16 is part of the solution. This chapter begins its exploration with a simple question: What types of inequality in voting across demographic categories are acceptable, and which are problematic? It discusses the reasons why it is problematic that not all demographic groups in the electorate vote in equal proportion. We seek to see which, if any, groups that vote at low levels are deserving of causing a reformation of our electoral processes. We will describe the gaps and their causes along with the most common prescriptions that have been proposed. We will discuss in order:

- European democracies voting at higher rates than in the United States.
- Richer Americans voting at higher rates than Americans with less wealth and income.
- Older Americans voting at higher rates than younger Americans.
- More-educated Americans voting at higher rates than less-educated Americans.

This last subject of inequality in education will be incorporated into the last section of the chapter which puts college education under closer scrutiny. This is not only because I am an educator, but also because education is a key to the transformation from little-j justice to Big-J Justice.

POLITICAL INEQUALITY—SOURCES, CONSEQUENCES, AND SOLUTIONS

Liberal democracy is predicated on essential equality. It is essential for a representative government to be accountable to its citizens through elections. The Lincolnian statement 'government of the people, by the people, for the people' captures the ideal. We have seen how American history has fallen short of this ideal, but that over time we have made impressive strides moving from what historian Allan Lichtman termed "A White Man's Republic" to our increasingly diverse electorate of today.[5] Because voting is the *sine qua non* of democracy, inequality in voting strikes at the heart of representative democracy. A famous saying is *one person one vote*. The most powerful CEO's vote counts no more than the vote of the homeless woman executing her civic duty.

Equality is necessary but not sufficient for categorizing a political system as a liberal democracy. Without regular, free, and open elections governments escape accountability and tend toward authoritarianism. The world is full of "democratic" states that do not respect individual rights or the rule of law. The phrase "one man, one vote, one time" captures the fallacy of believing that elections alone are sufficient to call a political system a liberal democracy.[6] These illiberal democracies are beyond the scope of this book. Our concern here is on how liberal democracies can extend their laws of suffrage to incorporate new voters and in the process, inject a needed jolt of equality and energy.

The practical impact of voting inequality is that some groups of citizens get more attention from politicians than others. An example is that since older citizens vote at higher rates than younger citizens, democratic political systems attend to the political demands of the elderly more than they respond to the demands and needs of the young.[7] Martin Wattenberg collected data from a wide range of surveys that show other areas where young and old citizens tend to take different positions, including guns, stock market holdings, employment searches, paying off student loans, and having gay friends.[8] In the words of two scholars, "Extensive research has shown that turnout inequalities shape not only who gets elected but also what policies get enacted."[9] A report about the global well-being of children discusses how President Johnson's War on Poverty succeeded in reducing elderly poverty in the United States by two-thirds to a point where only 9.1 percent are in poverty, while the numbers for children remain essentially unchanged with about 20 percent in poverty. According to Carolyn Miles who is the president and CEO of Save the Children, "Kids don't vote. There's definitely that difference in political power."[10]

We can see inequalities in voting rates at the international level with some countries having much higher turnout rates than other equally democratic states. For example, well-established European democracies typically have very much higher voter turnout rates than does the United States.[11] For example, drawing on data from International IDEA to look at just the most recent elections in the United States, France (presidential), Germany, and the United Kingdom, we see Germany at 76.2 percent in 2017; France at 74.6 percent in 2017; United Kingdom at 67.6 percent in 2019; and the United States at 58.8 percent in 2018.[12] If we look at the previous Presidential election in 2016, the United States' rate was 65.4 percent.

When seeking to explain the gap in voting rates between the United States and European democracies, attention immediately turns to elements of the voting process that differ. In other words, some of the peculiar features of American elections are seen to contribute to low voting rates. In the words of Green and Shachar, the low American voting rates might not be an expression of the rationality of American voters as much as it is "a historical by-product of efforts decades ago to discourage mass mobilization."[13] What then, can be done to fix this?

A number of scholars have identified commonsense reforms that could increase the voting rate and some have been implemented in certain localities.[14] Prescriptions tend to focus on standard reforms to the American political process, and these include, but are by no means limited to:

- Weekend voting—Very clearly, scheduling the election day on Tuesday without attaching it to any sort of holiday was not calculated to maximize voting rates. The negative impact of this has been muted by instituting early voting periods that make it much more convenient for voters to find the time to vote. Because of state control of elections, thus far only 39 states offer this very convenient option.[15] Not surprisingly, there have been controversies whenever state governments decide to shorten the days or hours that early voting is open.[16]
- Automatic Registration—The United States moved in this direction with the National Voter Registration Act of 1993 (popularly known as the Motor-Voter Act). This federal legislation made it possible for citizens to register to vote while taking care of other business at certain government offices, including where driver's licenses are processed. It is worth noting that linking voter registration opportunities to driver's licenses introduces a bias into the process by giving advantages to those with automobiles.[17] Several democracies make voter registration an automatic process conducted by the government.[18] Whenever a citizen reaches voting age their name is put onto voting rolls. This would undoubtedly increase voting because it would significantly reduce the costs of voting. A word of caution is necessary here. Empirical evidence suggests that simply reducing the costs of voting might not automatically increase voting rates. Holbein and Hillygus argue that young people have strong intentions to vote, but often do not manage to actually vote.[19] Rather than focus on the costs facing those young citizens, they focus on the young citizens themselves, specifically their non-cognitive skills. Rather than emphasizing political knowledge in civics courses, they encourage a shift to more practical knowledge. See chapter 5 for more discussion of civics.
- Changes in how votes are counted determine who wins—The United States generally employs the first-past-the-post election system, which essentially means whoever gets the most votes wins, even if the top candidate receives less than 50 percent of the vote. This means that a majority of the voters do

not get their preference. In our two-party political system, this is a limited problem. It only occurs whenever multiple candidates are competing—such as in primary contests and in some local elections. As Americans segregate themselves into Red and Blue housing patterns, and as politicians maneuver to create non-competitive congressional districts, primaries are becoming increasingly important, which makes solutions more attractive.

There are several options that are being pushed for adoption and there are some jurisdictions where new voting rules are already being implemented. The most popular one appears to be Instant Runoff Voting.[20] In this system, voters cast two or more votes in order of preference, and the votes that were cast for the candidates with the fewest votes are redistributed to other candidates among those who made the cut. So, for instance, if you wanted Jones to win in a 5-candidate race, and none of the candidates got a majority, and your candidate Jones finished 5th, your second preference would automatically be given your vote in what would be a second round of voting.

Lijphart maintained that our political system's claim to be representative was belied by the inequalities that are large by the standards of other advanced democracies. At the heart of his critique is the understanding that "if you do not vote you do not count."[21] A former politician expressed the same sentiment in a more colorful way, "Elected officials pay as much attention to those who are not registered to vote as butchers do to the food preferences of vegetarians."[22] Because he saw the inequalities as intrinsic to the American political system, Lijphart concluded that compulsory voting would be the most effective way to overcome this problem. This route, though not impossible, is unlikely because in the American political culture, the high value placed on freedom exceeds the value society attaches to maximizing political participation through voting. Moreover, as author Milner says, "If merely boosting turnout were our objective, we would ignore civic education in favor of compulsory voting. But our ultimate objective is informed political participation."[23]

Since the *de jure* voting restrictions have been removed from most groups (not including felons), we would expect that the voting rates would even out. Yet the inequality of participation rates persists. Hidden behind the benevolent picture of *de jure* equality is another picture of *de facto* inequality that sometimes seems as if Lijphart is correct and inequality is baked into our political system and beyond remedy short of radical transformation. While the diversity of the electorate has certainly risen over the years, there remain legacies of the past that are visible in turnout data. We can readily see that within the United States some types of people vote at higher rates than others. In the United States, people who fit the following characteristics are more likely to vote than those without these characteristics: Rich; White; Educated; Old.

Without making too fine a point on this, it is not surprising to find that the socioeconomic elite dominate in the voting realm as well. There are two examples, however, where the formerly disempowered groups have essentially caught up. One example is gender. Males, the traditionally privileged gender, now trail the female gender in voting rates though it took decades for this to happen.[24] The gap did not appear immediately because women did not have the habit of voting at first. As soon as a generation had cycled through, women began voting at higher rates than men. And that gap is widening with time. Using data going back to the 1964 elections, women had a very slight advantage of 61.9 percent turnout for women versus 61.5 percent turnout for men. In 2016, women voted at a 63.3 percent rate compared to 59.3 percent rate for men.[25]

The second instance is race. Much to the surprise of many, the racial gap in American voting is virtually nonexistent between African Americans and White Americans although widening relative to Hispanic and Asian. African Americans vote at higher rates than White Americans at all levels of education, yet African Americans have overall lower rates of voting because college-educated African Americans are a lower percentage of the overall African American population than is the case with college-educated Whites.[26] Because non-college-educated African Americans vote at low levels (as do non-college-educated White Americans), this reduces the overall African American voting rate.

This might be easier to see in a table. Imagine a hypothetical case where there are 100 African American eligible voters and 100 White American eligible voters. If we divide them according to high and low educational levels and then assign them different voting rates, we might see something like Table 3.1. In the example, both high education groups vote at higher percentages than do the low educational level groups. White Americans have a higher percentage of citizens in the high education groups. African Americans vote at higher rates than White Americans at both educational levels (100 percent–90 percent at high levels; 50 percent–20 percent at the low levels.) When we do the math, we see that 70 African Americans would vote, while 76 White Americans would vote.

But, are the inequalities that persist after the artificial barriers are removed, problematic? It can be argued that if everyone is equally allowed to vote, then any variance is a natural product of individual choices freely made, and thus are not of concern to the political system. All social life is characterized by inequality. Think for only a moment about your family, your school, your job, your favorite sports teams, and many other realms. In most of these cases there is some sort of hierarchy, oftentimes with true decision-making power concentrated at the top. Yet we generally accept these inequalities, though most of us chafe now and again against the decisions made by those above

Table 3.1 Voting Rates and Education (Hypothetical)

	Black Americans			White Americans		
	Percentage of Voters	*Voting Rate*	*Total Votes*	*Percentage of Voters*	*Voting Rate*	*Total Votes*
High Education Level	40	100	40	80	90	72
Low Education Level	60	50	30	20	20	4
Total Votes			70			76

Source: Produced by author.

us in these hierarchies. But, in a political democracy equality is different. In fact, it is particularly prized.

Political philosopher John Rawls' great "Veil of Ignorance" notion generated certain principles about the type of inequality that we should allow in our society.[27] The Veil deprives us of knowing our place in society. If we do not know whether we are White or not, male or not, rich or not, educated or not, then we would not want any variance in political power across those pairings. Historically, of course, each of these pairings has been associated with political inequalities—frequently established by law. Rawls postulated that the only acceptable inequalities are those that benefit the poorest in society. So, for example, it would be fine to pay our top political leader billions of dollars if that leader delivered an improved life for all. Another stipulation is that inequality is only acceptable if it is not based on some non-meritocratic characteristic. Thus, modern Rawlsian democracies agree that men should not automatically have more power than women. And, Whites should not automatically have more power than non-Whites.

What inequalities in voting would we, in a Rawlsian world, embrace? Primary suspects are gender, race, wealth, age, and education. We will not discuss the gender and racial imbalances much but will spend more time with the other imbalances.

The argument over gender inequality in voting seems moot since the previously excluded females currently outvote (meaning voting at higher rates) males. The margin is slight and is currently within acceptable bounds, and it is hard to imagine what factors lead to the decline in male voting.

Racial imbalances in voting present an interesting case. As noted earlier, African Americans outvote White Americans at every level of education. However, overall African Americans do not outvote White Americans. This connects to the inequality in education, where more-educated people outvote less-educated people. And as we will see shortly, college education is related to income and wealth. The solution for this, would seem to be economic in content. Until African Americans attain the income/wealth status of White Americans we can expect their educational attainment to lag and consequently their voting rates to lag.

INEQUALITY: ECONOMICS

Voting rights have been connected to economics going back at least as far as the widespread property-owning requirement. A justification for accepting that the rich will vote at higher rates than the less wealthy, would be that people with more money have a greater stake in society than those without as much money. This seems like an archaic explanation that your modestly paid author rejects. One could even argue that we would expect the poor to vote at higher rates in order to put into effect redistribution of wealth policies.

Economic standing has a direct impact on voting rates and indirect impact on voting through its relationship with education, which also impacts voting rates. Economic inequality has been growing in the United States and many other democracies during the same period that overall voting rates have declined, suggesting that the two might be connected. Solt performed a cross-national analysis of the cause of the economic gap in voting rates to test three theories to explain why economic inequality should generate differing voting rates.[28] The relative power theory postulates that inequality reduces incentives for poorer voters to bother with voting. The poor see the game as organized to benefit those at the top, and voting is unlikely to change anything, therefore why bother going through the trouble of voting? The conflict theory says that if inequality is high, then mobilization of voters should rise and the ballot will be a perfect place for the opposing sides to battle, leading to rising voting rates. The resource theory predicts that as society grows more unequal, the resources available to the poorest voters will decrease and they will be less likely to pay the "costs" of voting. Conversely, the rich will have more resources to expend, and therefore they will be more eager to pay the costs of voting. According to this theory, the impact on voting rates will vary while each group will trend in opposite directions. However, if the rich are in the minority, the overall impact on voting rates should be downward.

Solt reached broad conclusions on the unequivocally negative impact on voting rates caused by economic inequality. He said, "That economic inequality depresses political engagement, and especially that of people with lower incomes, has important implications for our understanding of political participation, of the politics of redistribution, and of democracy."[29] He added, "Greater economic inequality increasingly stacks the deck of democracy in favor of the richest citizens, and as a result, most everyone else is more likely to conclude that politics is simply a game not worth playing."[30] He reached the conclusion that of the three theories the relative power theory is consistent with his data. He concluded that the poor believe they lack political power and therefore they turn out to vote only rarely, and this explains why redistribution policies are rarely even on the agenda of democracies.[31] Fraga arrived at a similar conclusion. Variation of African American voting rates across time and different elections seems correlated with the closeness of the election.[32] This outcome is consistent with the rational actor model.

INEQUALITY: AGE

As we have already seen, age is another important element that emerges as a powerful explanatory variable when we look at recent decades. It certainly can be argued that old people know more about politics and how the world works than do younger people. This seems to the author to be true beyond debate. It seems natural that older citizens would vote at higher levels for a variety of obvious reasons. Greater knowledge of politics and the role of government, as well as greater investment in the community and greater concern with such matters as taxes, are clear examples. What we would not want is younger citizens voting at lower rates than younger citizens did a generation before.

In explaining low and declining voting rates, many point out the great disparity in voting across generations, with the older generations voting at much higher rates than younger generations.[33] Wattenberg and others point out that younger cohorts vote at lower levels than older cohorts, and lower than earlier cohorts when they were young.[34] Young people began voting in smaller numbers beginning in the 1970s after being largely equal to older voters before then.[35] This is significant because it shows that today's low-voting youth are not going to grow into high-voting adults. This explains the general downward trend in recent elections and portends a continuing decline in voting as lower-turnout generations continually replace higher-turnout generations.

Wattenberg, by focusing on age, misses some important implications. But his equation is simple and powerful and worth discussing. He seeks to explain the varying turnout levels by age, and he uses political knowledge as his main explanatory variable. After all, young people do not fail to vote because they are young. Citizens with little political knowledge tend to have low voting rates, and young people are particularly low on political knowledge. This also makes intuitive sense. Those who are less knowledgeable about politics are probably less interested in politics, and are thus less inclined to vote. Wattenberg emphasizes the lack of political knowledge with a chapter titled, "Don't Ask Anyone Under 30." He maintains that we should try to increase the political knowledge of young people, but he acknowledges this is difficult to achieve. This moves him to embrace the idea of compulsory voting.

HIGHER EDUCATION UNDER THE MICROSCOPE

We continue by discussing the state of matters in terms of the relationship of education and this book's proposal. One of the prominent and essential features of the proposal is that it will, in no small measure, address one of the inequalities in American politics. Everyone in college knows, or believes, or hopes that there is a strong and positive relationship between education and many positive social outcomes. Examples in support of this can readily be drawn from the fields of economics, psychology, and sociology, among others. Voting and other forms of political participation are prominent among these positive outcomes. The interest of political scientists in this topic can be traced as far back as 1924, leading someone to claim that "the relationship between education and turnout ranks among the most extensively documented correlations in American survey research."[36] At the same time, scholars of political engagement have long placed their hopes on civics courses in public schools to provide citizens with the tools and values that would prepare them to play active roles as citizens. Unfortunately, the news from the scholarship front is surprisingly, and disappointingly, negative, as we will see in Chapter 5.

The inequality is that citizens with more education vote (and engage in other political activities) at higher rates than citizens with less education, or as the immortal words of E.E. Schattschneider, "The flaw in the pluralist heaven is that the heavenly chorus sings with a strong upper-class accent."[37] This inequality is found across most of the democratic world, but expresses itself with particular force in the United States.[38]

When discussing education gaps there are two types that are distinct, but intertwined. The one that is most directly interesting to us is the voting gap that exists between citizens of different educational levels. The more educated, the more likely someone is to be a regular voter. The second gap refers to who attends college and who does not attend college. The idea of public universities supported by tax-payer's money is to provide equal access to the credentials, skills, and knowledge to be successful. It is supposed to be the great equalizer. It has not quite fulfilled its mission.

There are two important points to make about college education. The first is that college students (who will soon be likely voters) tend to be Whiter and richer than their non-college-age cohorts.[39] The second point is that college education is becoming increasingly expensive, and more and more lower- and working-class families are questioning whether the growing student debt levels are worth the investment. If these two trends persist then the educational gap in college attendance will grow even more widely than currently.[40]

The data is uneven and varies depending on whether college attendance or graduation is being measured. As every college student can attest, there is a big difference between the two. If we focus on attendance the news is generally positive. The percentage of college students from the bottom 20 percent is rising. When we look at graduation rates, the picture is mixed. The percentage of bottom 20 percent graduating from college has risen since the 1970s. That is good, but the percentage of the top 20 percent graduating has risen considerably faster. Thus, the educational gap in graduation rates across economic levels continues to widen.[41] Add the growing inequality, as wealth becomes more unequal, and education will be expected to follow suit.

Even public education has rarely been free. The North Carolina constitution since 1869 reads:

> The General Assembly shall provide that the benefits of The University of North Carolina and other public institutions of higher education, as far as practicable, be extended to the people of the State free of expense.[42]

The University of North Carolina - Chapel Hill's original tuition was $8 when it opened in 1795 ($186 today). UNC-Chapel Hill's tuition and fees in 2019 was $8987 per year (excluding books and living expenses). Today, three UNC system universities offer tuition of $500 a semester (fees and living expenses are extra). Fees and living expenses of course make the final price tag much higher than $500 a semester. High enough to make families wonder if a college degree has that much value. It does, but student educational debt is a troublesome problem.

Not surprisingly, as much else in the world, individual colleges are not equal in terms of who gets admitted and who graduates. When we analyze the impact of education we recognize that the gap not only exits, it is widening. As with credential inflation (today's bachelor's degree is the equivalent of yesterday's high school diploma) those with less education are being left behind. We cannot simply wait for everyone to get a college degree for a couple of reasons. First, that is not likely to happen. Second, if the impact of college is through the status that it conveys to the degree holder, then we would expect that a graduate degree will become the dividing educational line between high and low voters.

One of the trends that has been discovered is that in the last decade the number of students from poor backgrounds attending the most prestigious public colleges has been declining in terms of the percentage of overall students. Thus, the best public institutions are catering more and more to the richest young people. Some important state universities are moving in opposite directions. One case is the University of Alabama which decided to increase the amount of the scholarships given based on merit and allocates around $100 million in financial aid to students who lack financial need.[43] At first blush, this sounds very appropriate but it has an underappreciated side effect. Awarding scholarships to those who score the highest on academic measures, rather than based on financial need, tends to reward students who are not necessarily inherently better students, but those who happen to be fortunate enough to attend better elementary and high schools and get more academic attention that other youth. Thus, awarding finite scholarship dollars in meritocratic fashion has the effect of transferring the benefits from those who need it the most, to those who are likely to have had more fortunate backgrounds. This type of decision contributes to the erosion of the faith that college is the great equalizer. This concern is also driven by ever-rising costs of higher education which naturally hits the least economically secure students the hardest. The news is not all bad. By contrast, the University of Pittsburgh has cut back on its merit scholarship funding and shifted it toward matching Pell Grants with the goal of meeting the student's actual educational needs.[44] In a similar fashion the University of Utah is planning to phase out merit scholarships entirely.[45] In its place, it will provide scholarships to students whose families earn less than $50,000 a year.

Burd also found that the educational gap in college attendance is steadily expanding.[46] Among his findings are that low-income students succeed when they matriculate into top-tier academic institutions but those institutions are admitting fewer lower-income students and expanding the numbers they admit from the top 20 percent of income. Pfeffer conducted a survey of cohorts born in the 1970s and 1980s in 20 advanced democratic economies and concluded that the educational attainment of parents accounted for the educational gap in college attendance.[47] His concern is that this gap has been increasing at a time when the costs of higher education are climbing and the consequent risk of debt being incurred without a degree being conferred may be leading lower-income families to pass up collegiate opportunities. Rising inequality in higher education will predictably lead to lower voting rates.

While it is true that education is positively connected to voting, scholars cannot agree on why that is the case. And in the process, they discovered a puzzle about voting that makes answering the question of why this connection is very important. The puzzle is that the US population is constantly becoming more educated, yet the voting rate is flat or negative. It should be positive, since more-educated citizens vote more often than less-educated citizens.

Sondheimer and Green used longitudinal data to untangle this puzzle of declining voter turnouts while educational levels are increasing.[48] Their findings support the claim that the impact of college is real and not a spurious result. They speculate about the pathways by which this change in behavior is effected. Their results do not support any definitive conclusion but the two highest on the list of speculations are (1) More education leads to greater skills in navigating government bureaucracies thereby reducing the costs of voting; (2) More education leads to more political knowledge and interest.

The contested question of the mechanisms by which more education yields higher political participation can be divided into three broad perspectives.[49] The first focuses on a range of causes that have their impact prior to attending college. These include genetics, intelligence, parents, household wealth, and others. These explanations identify a correlation between those items and the decision to attend college. They claim that the factors that lead someone to attend college are the same as the ones that cause a college-educated citizen to become engaged in politics. Thus, for example, college-educated parents encourage their children to go to college and when they graduate they become engaged citizens. In this case, proto-voters pass through college, but the die is cast prior to those formative years.

The second type of explanations focus on what happens in college. They look at either the gain of political knowledge or of skills that would contribute to the political efficacy of college graduates. We also know that the choice of college major affects the likelihood of a college student or graduate to vote.[50] The political knowledge perspective is strengthened by the reliable results showing that social science and humanities majors are more politically engaged than are business and STEM (Science, Technology, Engineering, and Math) students. The political skills explanation also is consistent with those results since political engagement is intimately bound up with the use of words, the interpretation of meanings, and so forth. These are more prominently developed in the social science and humanities fields.

The third type of explanations focus on the status of those with college degrees. They find that political engagement is dominated by whoever is of the highest status. College then acts as a sorting mechanism, with graduates ready to join the elite while non-college graduates are not. The great virtue of this type of explanation is that it does account for the puzzle referred to earlier (that variables predicting high voting have been increasing, but voting has been decreasing). Not very long ago the high school degree was a leading indicator of elite status, and now the BA degree serves in that role. Thus, the percentages of Americans who are considered elite remain roughly the same, and the voting rates of the non-elites are considerably lower.

So, the first theory is that what happens before college matters, the second theory is what happens in college matters, and the third theory is what happens after college matters. This proposal interacts with these explanations in different ways. If we assume that the die is cast before college, then great positive value is placed on the revised active civics courses which would create some of the early formative experiences for those without strong familial backgrounds in political engagement.[51] If, on the other hand, the knowledge and skills that are gained in college are what explains college graduates being politically engaged, even STEM students would become more likely to vote after being taken through the registration and voting process in high school. If, however, college is mostly a status symbol, the proposed reform does not change as much. Not all high school students will be elites, even if they learn how to vote. Nonetheless, this proposal challenges the status quo relationship because if we can turn the non-elite into voters, then they can also have a strong political voice.

Regardless of where the origin of the change is located, it remains clear that college relates to increased political participation including voting. With college education being a transitional place with high political participation on one side and low participation rates on the other, the factors that influence who does and does not get a college degree become critically important.

Figure 3.1 shows the gap between the voting rates of Americans based on their educational levels.[52] The relationship is clean in the sense that none of the lines overlap. In other words, in every election from 1986 to 2018 the more highly educated voters have higher turnout rates than those with lesser education. If we look at the different education levels individually we see different patterns. The postgraduate citizens show steady rates or even slightly upward rates of voting. The change between the first mid-term (1986) and the last mid-term (2018) was positive at 7.7 percent. Making the same calculations for the first Presidential (1988) and the last Presidential (2016) elections, we see that the change was positive at 5.1 percent. Making the same calculations for the same College to College Grad comparison we see the mid-term gap to be positive at 4.7 percent, and for the presidential election the positive gain was 5.1 percent. The pattern reverses when we move to the

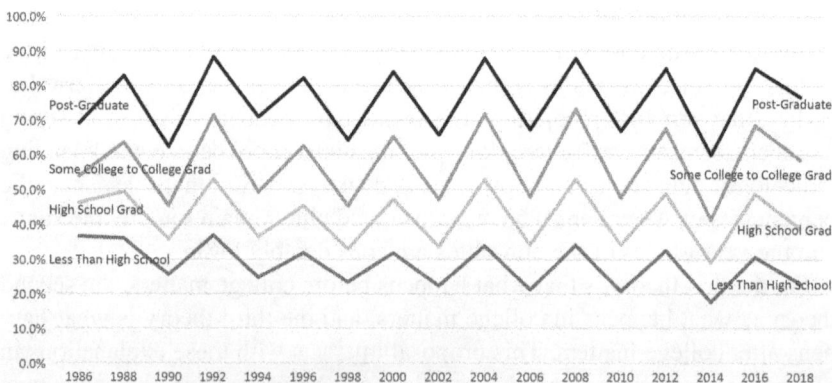

Figure 3.1   Turnout Rates by Education.

High School Grad with a slight decline over the period. For the mid-term, the decline was 7.2 percent, and for the presidential the decline was 0.5 percent. The greatest change however is among the Less Than High School citizens. For the mid-term gap the decline was a whopping 13.6 percentage points. For the presidential elections, the decline was 5.3 percent.

The education gap in voting is not only an American problem but the problem is very large in America. The United States stands out from other advanced democracies in the degree of inequality associated with the effects of education. Aina Gallego conducted calculations on 85 democratic elections in *Unequal Political Participation Worldwide.*[53] She shows that outside of compulsory voting countries, there are great variations in how unequal participation rates are based on education levels. This means that context can influence the degree of inequality; it is not an immutable feature of democracy, and low turnout rates are not an unalterable feature of the less educated. She concluded, "anything that makes voting more cognitively challenging will reduce the participation of less educated people disproportionately and will result in sharper turnout inequalities."[54] Gallego points out that burdensome registration/voting procedures harm younger and poorer voters more than they harm older and richer voters. "If policy makers or the public opinion decide—at some point and for whatever reason—that large inequalities in voter participation are unacceptable or undesirable, then a public debate can emerge on how to make participation more equal. Academics may have something important to add to this debate in the form of prescriptions."[55]

When we look at the age issue through the lens of education levels a very different picture emerges. We find that the decline in voting among younger cohorts is found primarily among the less-educated youth. College graduates do not exhibit the same decline in voting over time than citizens with less education exhibit. Blais *et al.* studied Canadian elections and attributed the decline almost entirely in the dipping turnout rates among the less-educated citizens.[56] They found that while overall voting rates were dropping well-educated citizens maintained their voting patterns. As with other democracies this occurred even as education rates were rising. This means that the decline is more serious among the less educated than it first appears.

Leightly and Nagler provide important data on this point. Comparing data from 1972 and 2008 shows the decline in voting across different educational levels.[57] In Table 3.2, if there was zero educational gap in turnout rates, each of the cells would be scored as 1.0. Numbers less than 1.0 indicate an educational category whose voting rate is less than their percentage of the voting age population. Numbers greater than 1.0 indicate an educational category whose voting rate is higher than their percentage of the voting age population.

Table 3.2 shows that in 1972 only the citizens without a high school degree voted at rates less than their percentage of the population. In 2008 that group

Table 3.2   **Voting Rates by Education Level**

Education	1972 Voting rate as percentage of Population rate	2008 Voting rate as percentage of Population rate	Difference
Less than High School	.79	.62	−.17
High School Graduate	1.03	.86	−.17
Some College	1.18	1.07	−.11
College Graduate	1.33	1.24	−.09

Source: Adapted from Leightly and Nagler, p. 36. Modified by author.

had been joined by high school graduates who were now voting at lower rates than their percentage of the population. Meanwhile the non-high school graduates declined even further. The positive news is that the percentage of the population with some college education or a college degree has grown substantially in the intervening 36 years, as is shown in Table 3.3.

This shows that the two underperforming voting categories now comprise a much smaller proportion of the overall population. The two overperforming voting categories now constitute a much larger proportion of the overall population. Leightly and Nagler show that the overall voting rate dropped from 63.6 percent in 1972 to 58.2 percent in 2008.[58] The implications of this are astounding. The overall American electorate is much more educated than in the past, but it does not vote at the same levels as previous electorates. The anticipated rise in voting rates due to the increases in the wealth, education, and age of the electorate is being counteracted by the decline of voting among those Americans with the least education. And this is occurring even as those less-educated Americans are declining as a percentage of the population. This is a very troubling development. The diagnosis of the puzzle of rising age and education with declining voting lands squarely in the laps of the less-educated White citizens. The more-educated citizens still vote at high rates. The solution as we shall soon see is Votes at 16.

When we apply the race variable to this educational variable an even more surprising result emerges. The educational gap in voting disappears among non-White groups, but remains powerful among Whites. Using Census data Fraga shows that for Whites with no high school degree the voting rate dropped from 52 percent to 40 percent between 1976 and 2016. By contrast, the same education group among African Americans rose from 48 percent to 53 percent over the same period.

Looked at from the perspective of the gaps between those with lowest education and highest education it is even more impressive. Table 3.4 shows that the gap among White Americans has grown substantially over the 1976–2016

Table 3.3   Education Rates as Percentage of Total Population

Education	1972 as percentage of total population	2008 as percentage of total population	Difference
Less than High School	36.6	11.2	−25.4
High School Graduate	37.5	31.7	−5.8
Some College	14.3	29.6	15.3
College Graduate	11.7	27.5	15.8

Source: Adapted by Leightly and Nagler, p. 36. Modified by author.

Table 3.4   Voting Rates by Race and Education

	African Americans			White Americans		
Education Levels	Highest Educated (%)	Lowest Educated (%)	Difference (%)	Highest Educated (%)	Lowest Educated (%)	Difference (%)
1976	84	48	36	88	52	36
2016	89	53	36	89	40	49

Source: Derived from data presented in Fraga. 2018, p. 60. Modified by author.

time period: from 36 percent to 49 percent. Among African Americans the gap between lowest and highest educated has remained constant over that 40-year period at 36 percent. This underlines the importance of education as an explanatory variable. But it is only among the White American population that the voting gap between highest and lowest is growing.[59]

CONCLUSION

This chapter emphasizes that our politics, as seen through the lens of voting rates, is clearly characterized by inequalities. It seems obvious that this is important and the reform proposed here will have some impact on these inequalities. The book's project is to show how lowering the voting age can mitigate some of these inequalities.

The decision to leave voting rights out of the Constitution (discussed in Chapter 2) meant that they would be decided in political contexts as well as in legal contexts and thereby guaranteeing that we would have constant struggles over who is allowed and who is not allowed to vote. Non-land owners were originally excluded from elections on the reasoning that they did not have the capability to embody the common good when they lacked the essence of what John Locke and others considered to be the prerequisites for citizenship.[60] Women and non-Whites were excluded because they were seen to be mentally and emotionally incapable of conducting responsible political thought. Some of the inequality present in today's America was deliberately installed in terms of the exclusion of the franchise from specific groups. The sad history of Jim Crow laws in the American South testifies to this. And the rush of southern states to begin implementing restrictions on voting rights immediately after the Supreme Court in 2013 removed the preclearance provision of the Voting Rights Act of 1965 illustrates the enduring power of this reasoning.[61] But, over the last 160 years we have expanded the electorate immensely, but not steadily.

We noted the voting gap between European and American voters. Moreover, Americans do not vote at high rates and the trends are downward. This led to prescriptions that focus on improving the way elections are run in the United States. By making the registration process easier, by moving the election day to the week end, and other assorted reforms, we would expect to raise the turnout rates across the entire electorate. Even if implemented and successful in the eyes of their advocates, we might expect to see voting rates increase in all categories. This is not actually true however, since making something marginally easier will not have as much effect on the groups that already vote at high rates in comparison to those groups that have low voting rates. Think of a rich person who sees that a pair of ear buds is $10 cheaper today, and then think of a smart, hard-working, but revenue-starved college student. Which person is more likely to change their behavior because of the discounted price? Consequently, these reforms, as limited as they may be, will reduce voting inequality to some degree. These reforms will be more likely to add more citizens from the low-voting categories than from the high-voting categories.

Minor reforms will not eliminate the age disparity that perplexes Wattenberg so much. His analysis moved the focus of the problem from how elections are run to how young people behave politically. As he noted, the way elections are being run has not gotten worse over the years; in fact, it is now easier for citizens to register, and in many states voting is now spread out over several days. Yet, voting rates have dropped and do not seem to be rising. The election results of 2018 may represent a change, but whether it is a temporary or permanent change is yet to be determined. So, if the problem is not the way we organize our elections, it must be something about potential voters that is the problem. Not reading newspapers or paying attention to news on a regular basis is Wattenberg's diagnosis. His prescription is compulsory voting. He sees little hope in any smaller reform to change the pattern that we see.

We can blame all young people, or we can check to see which young people are voting at low and/or dropping rates. Here we find out that it is the less-educated voters who are voting less. We can look inside that demographic and find out that it is White Americans with less than college education levels whose voting rates are declining. Analyzing citizens by age based on their average political knowledge revealed disparities across age groups. But it obscured the variance within age groups.

Other scholars like Aina Gallego, Russell Dalton and Leightly and Nagler tell us that the critical issue is not age, but education. And Fraga led us to understand that the problems appear to be confined to the less-educated White Americans. We also learned that the puzzle is not a puzzle when we recognize that the group that is not voting at the same rate as in the past is the least educated.

One conclusion derived from this chapter is that because economic inequalities lead to corresponding inequalities in education, unequal political participation will follow as will unequal political influence. Since economic inequality is a growing phenomenon in much of the advanced world, and has been a long-standing feature of capitalist economic systems, this problem is going to be with us for the foreseeable future. And, until college education is made free and available to all, educational inequalities are certain to remain. In fact, trends in higher education are leading to a wider educational gap in college attendance as state public institutions are becoming more expensive. One of the predictable outcomes is that more and more young people will find themselves on the wrong side of the educational divide when it comes to the likelihood of voting. This phenomenon is troubling because, unlike voting on Tuesdays or getting older, education has a strong connection with other social realms that are marked by inequality: specifically, wealth and race. College, for example, is skewed away from the overall population and toward the privileged groups. Despite efforts by land-grant universities and others, the college populations are whiter and richer than the average in America.

When I came across the education gap in voting in my early forays into the voting literature, I was very impressed, and my international proclivities led me to Aina Gallego's work describing and explaining how this is a transnational issue. Recognition that voting in the United States is unevenly spread across educational levels, followed by a realization that college education is highly stratified by economic class, and by race, made it imperative to take the matter seriously. It was not until later that I conceived of my proposal as a potential solution to this problem. The connection became clearer as I recognized the significance of the difference between those with more education and those with less education. As a college professor, I instinctively drew the line between high school and college. And I was aware of my university's efforts, and my own contributions to those, to encourage voting and political engagement to our students. Full disclosure: I have been involved with the American Democracy Project which is a program created and run by the American Association of State Colleges and Universities, and which has as its primary mission to support public higher education institutions to prepare college students and graduates for responsible citizenship.[62] Recognition that we were not providing the same encouragement to non-college students struck me hard. We were contributing to the inequality! Fortunately, this passing sense of guilt was replaced by a conviction that the proper answer is not to cease efforts to increase voting and political participation by college students, rather it is to increase the probability that non-college students will also increase their voting and political participation rates. After all, it is not the case that college students *vote too much.*

In this chapter, we identified the most important sources of political inequalities and introduced some proposed solutions. Foremost among the inequalities are these: Wealth/income; age; education levels. Just as these are interconnected in the sense that they are often found (or missing) in the same person, so also are the solutions interconnected. To solve the gap in economics requires someone else to figure out. To solve the education gap in voting we must overcome the education gap in college attendance. The key to this is to bring voting to citizens who are not old enough for college. To solve the age gap, the solution is also to bring voting to those who are collected together in high school. If we do these things, we will diminish the age gap in voting and see the education gap in voting also fade away.

This has taken us very far. By locating the problem of low and declining voting rates among the less-educated citizenry, we can consider options. We noted how the cost of college education is rising quickly and may be reducing the number of poor and working-class youth who might otherwise attend college. If all educational categories were dropping at the same rate, we have one type of problem. But if the drop is nearly all attributable to declines among a certain sub-group, we have a different type of problem. And different types of problems call for different types of solutions. When we can identify, as we have here, the problem with one segment of the overall population, we can fashion solutions specific to that segment of the population. In this case our analysis has shifted our focus to citizens without college degrees. And, because young citizens vote at lower rates than older citizens, we naturally focus our attention on young people who are not on track to become college graduates.

The solution to declining educational groups is to bring voting to them. How this will happen is the subject of Chapter 4. It involves discussions of costs and habits of voting. The voting rates (dropping and becoming more unequal) are problematic. Traditional solutions seem too tame and we want something adequate to the task. It has been suggested that Votes at 16 is the prescription that seems ideally suited for this.

To summarize: We do not see anything problematic with the gender imbalance. Racial imbalances are interesting because African Americans should have higher overall voting rates than White Americans. This is associated with wealth and with education. The economic imbalance is problematic and is associated with education. Age is not a problem unless it continues as cohorts get older. Education is the key imbalance and deserves great attention. Not everyone goes to college, and those that do, vote at higher rates than those who do not go to college.

NOTES

1. Lijphart, Arend. "Unequal Participation: Democracy's Unresolved Dilemma." *American Political Science Review* 91, no. 1 (1997): 1–14. https://www.jstor.org/sta ble/2952255?seq=1#metadata_info_tab_contents

2. Lijphart. "Unequal Participation," 2.

3. Lijphart. "Unequal Participation," 3.

4. Pew Research Center. "The Party of Nonvoters." U.S. Politics & Policy. *Pew Research Center*, October 31, 2014. https://www.people-press.org/2014/10/31/the-p arty-of-nonvoters-2/.

5. Lichtman. *The Embattled Vote in America*, 36–69.

6. Zakaria, Fareed. "The Rise of Illiberal Democracy." *Foreign Affairs* 76, no. 6 (December 1997): 22–43. https://www.foreignaffairs.com/articles/1997-11-01/rise -illiberal-democracy

7. Wattenberg. *Is Voting for Young People?*

8. Wattenberg. *Is Voting for Young People?*, 135.

9. Holbein and Hillygus. *Making Young Voters*, 5.

10. Mackinnon, Amy, and C. K. Hickey. "The Kids Aren't Alright." *Foreign Policy*, May 28, 2019. https://foreignpolicy.com/2019/05/28/us-ranks-with-china-in- child-well-being-save-the-children-end-of-childhood-report-2019/

11. Brechenmacher, Saskia. "Comparing Democratic Distress in The United States and Europe." *Carnegie Endowment for International Peace*, June 2018. https://ca rnegieendowment.org/files/CP_337_Saskia_Full_FINAL.pdf

12. "Voter Turnout Database." Data. *International IDEA*. Accessed March 8, 2020. https://www.idea.int/data-tools/data/voter-turnout

13. Green, Donald P., and Ron Schachar. "Habit Formation and Political Behaviour: Evidence of Consuetude in Voter Turnout." *British Journal of Political Science* 30, no. 4 (October 2000): 561–73. https://www.cambridge.org/core/journals/british-journal -of-political-science/article/habit-formation-and-political-behaviour-evidence-of-con suetude-in-voter-turnout/4F834B816865D4ED0CE7EEB6C0A710CF, 572.

14. Hart and Youniss. *Renewing Democracy in Young America*; and Lawless and Fox. *Running From Office.*

15. National Conference of State Legislatures. "State Laws Governing Early Voting." Non-Profit. *NCSL*, August 2, 2019. https://www.ncsl.org/research/elections- and-campaigns/early-voting-in-state-elections.aspx

16. Lopez, German. "7 Specific Ways States Made It Harder for Americans to Vote in 2016." Political. *Vox*, 07 2016. https://www.vox.com/policy-and-politics/ 2016/11/7/13545718/voter-suppression-early-voting-2016

17. Highton, Benjamin, and Raymond E. Woflinger. "Estimating the Effects of the National Voter Registration Act of 1993." *Political Behavior* 20, no. 2 (1998): 79–104. https://link.springer.com/article/10.1023%2FA%3A1024851912336

18. Lichtman. *The Embattled Vote in America*, 239–40.

19. Holbein and Hillygus. *Making Young Voters*, ch. 1, 1–21.

20. Amy, Douglas J. "Instant Runoff Voting." Political. FairVote, February 15, 2020. https://www.fairvote.org/instant_runoff_voting_no_substitute_for_pr

21. Lijphart. "Unequal Participation," 4. Quoting Walter Dean Burnham.

22. Holbein and Hillygus. *Making Young Voters,* 5. Barney Frank quoted, 6.

23. Milner. *The Internet Generation*, 195.

24. Leighley, Jan E., and Jonathan Nagler. *Who Votes Now?: Demographics, Issues, Inequality and Turnout in the United States*, 78. Princeton, NJ: Princeton University Press, 2014.

25. Center for American Women and Politics. "Gender Differences in Voter Turnout." Eagleton Institute of Politics: Rutgers University, September 16, 2019. https://cawp.rutgers.edu/sites/default/files/resources/genderdiff.pdf

26. Fraga, Bernard L. *The Turnout Gap: Face, Ethnicity, and Political Inequality in a Diversifying America*, 20–52. Cambridge, UK: Cambridge University Press, 2018, ch. 2.

27. Rawls. *A Theory of Justice*, 3–46. Revised. Cambridge, MA: Harvard University Press, 1999, ch. 1.

28. Solt, Frederick. "Economic Inequality and Democratic Political Engagement." *American Journal of Political Science* 52, no. 1 (January 2008): 48–60. https://www.jstor.org/stable/25193796?seq=1#metadata_info_tab_contents

29. Solt. "Economic Inequality and Democratic Political Engagement," 57.

30. Solt. "Economic Inequality and Democratic Political Engagement," 58.

31. Solt. "Economic Inequality and Democratic Political Engagement," 57.

32. Fraga. *The Turnout Gap*, 83–6.

33. Gallego. "Where Else Does Turnout Decline Come from?"; and Solt. "Economic Inequality and Democratic Political Engagement."

34. Wattenberg. *Is Voting for Young People?* ch.4, 89–118.

35. Wattenberg. *Is Voting for Young People?*, 117.

36. Sondheimer, Rachel Milstein, and Donald P. Green. "Using Experiments to Estimate the Effects of Education on Voter Turnout." *American Journal of Political Science* 54, no. 1 (January 2010): 174–89. https://onlinelibrary.wiley.com/doi/full/10.1111/j.1540-5907.2009.00425.x, 174.

37. Schattschneider, Elmer Eric. *The Semi-Sovereign People: A Realist's View of Democracy in America*, 35. Boston, MA: Wadsworth, 1960.

38. Gallego, Aina. *Unequal Political Participation Worldwide*, 1–34. New York, NY: Cambridge University Press, 2015, ch. 1.

39. Carnevale, Anthony P., Megan L. Fasules, Michael C. Quinn, and Kathryn Peltier Campbell. "Born to Win, Schooled to Lose: Why Equally Talented Students Don't Get Equal Chances to Be All They Can Be." *Georgetown University Center on Education and the Workforce*, 2019. https://cew.georgetown.edu/cew-reports/schooled2lose/

40. Burd, Stephen. "Moving On Up?" *New America*, October 2017, 2–57. https://na-production.s3.amazonaws.com/documents/Moving-on-Up.pdf

41. Pfeffer, Fabian T. "Persistent Inequality in Educational Attainment and Its Institutional Context." *European Sociological Review* 24, no. 5 (May 2008): 543–65. https://www.jstor.org/stable/25209187?seq=1#metadata_info_tab_contents

42. North Carolina General Assembly, "Article IX Education," 1971. https://www.ncleg.gov/Laws/Constitution/Article9.

43. Burd. "Moving On Up?", 6.

44. St. Amour, Madeline. "New Grant Program at Pitt Matches Pell Grants and Targets Students' Unmet Need." *Inside Higher Ed*, October 18, 2019. https://www.insidehighered.com/print/news/2019/10/18/new-grant-program-pitt-matches-pell-grants-and-targets-students-unmet-need

45. Johnson, Elin. "Utah to Phase Out Merit Scholarships." *Inside Higher Ed*, Quick Takes, November 25, 2019. https://www.insidehighered.com/quicktakes/2019/11/25/utah-phase-out-merit-scholarships#.Xk__V7OZe1A.link

46. Burd. "Moving On Up?", 21.

47. Pfeffer. "Persistent Inequality in Educational Attainment," 562–4.

48. Sondheimer and Green. "Using Experiments to Estimate the Effects of Education on Voter Turnout," 175.

49. Persson, Mikael. "Education and Political Participation." *British Journal of Political Science* 45, no. 3 (July 2015): 689–703. https://www.cambridge.org/core/journals/british-journal-of-political-science/article/education-and-political-participation/D17F1067290DFBEB1EC01F8B4C166C28

50. Hillygus, D. Sunshine. "The Missing Link: Exploring the Relationship Between Higher Education and Political Engagement." *Political Behavior* 27, no. 1 (March 2005): 25–47. https://link.springer.com/article/10.1007%2Fs11109-005-3075-8

51. Perrin, Andrew J., and Alanna Gillis. "How College Makes Citizens: Higher Education Experiences and Political Engagement." *Socius: Sociological Research for a Dynamic World* 5 (2019): 1–16. https://journals.sagepub.com/doi/10.1177/2378023119859708

52. McDonald, Michael P. "United States Election Project: Voter Turnout Demographics."

53. Gallego. *Unequal Political Participation Worldwide*.

54. Gallego. *Unequal Political Participation Worldwide*, 195.

55. Gallego. *Unequal Political Participation Worldwide*, 194.

56. Blais, Andre, Elisabeth Gidengil, and Neil Nevitte. "Where Does Turnout Decline Come From?" *European Journal of Political Research* 43, no. 2 (Fall 2004): 221–36. https://onlinelibrary.wiley.com/doi/full/10.1111/j.1475-6765.2004.00152.x

57. Leighley and Nagler. *Who Votes Now?*, 36.

58. Leighley and Nagler. *Who Votes Now?*, 21.

59. Fraga. *The Turnout Gap*, 60.

60. Lichtman. *The Embattled Vote in America*. 14.

61. Alexander, Michelle. *The New Jim Crow: Mass Incarceration in the Age of Colorblindness*, 1–43. New York, NY: The New Press, 2012, especially ch. 1.

62. "American Democracy Project." Educational. American Association of State Colleges and Universities. Accessed March 5, 2020. https://www.aascu.org/programs/ADP/

Chapter 4

Nurturing Lifetime Habits of Voting

INTRODUCTION: HOW THE 26TH
AMENDMENT GOT PASSED

The first three chapters have been building the case for Votes at 16, but there is one important piece missing. We have discussed the weaknesses of the instinctive criticisms of this reform and we have explored the empirical case built from the locations where Votes at 16 is in place. We surveyed the political history of voting in the United States to find the connections between our proposal and the trends in our history. And we examined the political inequality that shapes the political context for this proposed change. Now we turn to the final piece of the puzzle. How will the reform avoid replicating the declining voting rates that occurred when we last dropped the voting age? The answer is rooted in the error that was made in changing the voting age in 1971, and in the way in which citizens can become habitual voters.

Our story begins with the adoption of the 26th Amendment in 1971. Sometimes turbulent political times engender frantic attempts to provide a fix. Political reforms completed in haste may be wise or unwise, but they are likely to have unanticipated consequences. Looking back at the extraordinarily rapid passage of the 26th Amendment dropping the minimum voting age from 21 to 18, we can evaluate the wisdom of that reform while considering some of the unexpected ramifications.

Here are some basic facts about the 26th Amendment whose ratification was completed on July 1, 1971, a mere 100 days after it was proposed by Congress. Among other notable features, this amendment was the fastest ever approved. The vote in the House of Representatives was 401-19, followed quickly by passage in the Senate by a unanimous vote of 94-0. On the very day that Congress proposed the Amendment, March 23, 1971, five state

legislatures approved it. Another six legislatures passed it by the end of the
month, and the Amendment reached its required three-quarters threshold for
ratification on July 1, 1971, with the passage by the North Carolina legislature. By October 4, 1971, 42 states had ratified it, with South Dakota ratifying
it in 2014. Seven states have yet to act on the Amendment.[1]

Part of the astounding success came from President Nixon supporting and
then celebrating the passage of the Amendment. Of course, Presidents have
no formal authority in the amendment process with the power allocated to
the Congress and the states. So, it was necessary for Congress to embrace the
Amendment. Thus, in many ways the 26th Amendment can be seen as a product of the war, specifically, the anti-war contingent in Congress. Nonetheless,
having a Republican president be a strong advocate for the Amendment certainly helped.

For our purposes here, the concern is not with the debates that gave rise
to this Amendment except to the degree that its advocates advanced grand,
but not irrational, claims. Advocates relied on a combination of normative
and empirical arguments. The normative arguments were dominant, as it was
claimed that drafting young men to fight in Vietnam without allowing them
to vote was unjust. In this way society could, in essence, repay that generation for the drafting of some of them to fight in Vietnam, by extending the
rights of suffrage to them. The second argument was not as prominent but
might have been an essential part of the process. It maintained that this highly
energized generation would vote at high levels. Thus, where one argument
aimed to repay the youth for Vietnam, the other was hoping that the youth
would redeem the political system that seemed to be in great trouble. The
political class knew that this generation was politically engaged to a fault.
The problem, as they saw it, was that the youth were not "working within
the system" and instead working to destroy the system. From this perspective, the 26th Amendment made this a realistic possibility for college-age
students.

The purpose of this brief recap of the winning arguments on behalf of the
26th Amendment is to set the context for its rapid passage that was supported
by President Nixon. This is important because as we will see, this hopeful
change was not rewarded with the explosion (peaceful) of youthful engagement with the electoral processes. Instead, it laid the groundwork for declining voting rates in the United States since it was instituted.

Little did we know that this was going to set up the current and succeeding
generations for low voting rates. Prior to the passage of this amendment the
gap between the youngest and oldest eligible cohorts was relatively minor,
but that gap was set to increase as more and more younger voters entered the
electorate. Using updated data from Marin Wattenberg, we see the following
pattern.[2]

In interpreting this data, we must take care to understand that in the elections prior to 1972 the youngest voting cohort was 21–24.[3] Thereafter it switched to 18–24. The ratio column indicates how much more likely someone in the first category (65+) is to vote compared to someone in the second category (21–24). So, in 1964 the 65+ were 30 percent more likely to vote than the 21–24-year-olds. By 2016, this had climbed to 70 percent more likely to vote. The highest age category was 45–64 for the period 1964–1984, but since then the 65+ age group has voted at the highest rates. It may be saying too much, but this looks like the senior citizens voted themselves secure retirements though the ballot box.

Turning to mid-term elections where turnouts are always much lower, the pattern in Table 4.2 is similar to Table 4.1, but the ratio numbers are much more pronounced.[4] This indicates that in the mid-term elections the gap between the oldest voters and the youngest is much larger. For example, only in the Presidential elections years of 1996 and 2000 was the ratio as high as 2.1 (meaning that older voters were twice as likely to vote as the youngest voters). By contrast only the 1970 mid-term election was less than that (1.9) and only two were at 2.1 (1966, and 2018), while the other elections were higher. It is worth noting that the 1966 and 1970 years where youth did relatively well (talk about grade inflation!) were prior to the dropping of the voting age to 18.

All of this makes the 2018 results especially important.[5] The numbers are striking. Looking at the gaps between 2014 and 2018 we can appreciate the magnitude of the increased voting rates in 2018. What is especially significant to our project is that the biggest jump between mid-term elections, by far, was among the 18–24-year-olds. That increase was nearly doubled, with

Table 4.1 Voting Rates in Presidential Election Years 1964–2016, in percentages

	18–24	25–44	45–64	65+	Ratio: 65+:18–24
1964	50.9	69.0	75.9	66.3	1.3
1968	50.4	66.6	74.9	65.8	1.3
1972	49.6	62.7	70.8	63.5	1.3
1976	42.2	58.7	68.7	62.2	1.5
1980	39.9	58.7	69.3	65.1	1.6
1984	40.8	58.4	69.8	67.7	1.7
1988	36.2	54.0	67.9	68.8	1.9
1992	42.8	58.3	70.0	70.1	1.6
1996	32.4	49.2	64.4	67.0	2.1
2000	32.3	49.8	64.1	67.6	2.1
2004	41.9	52.2	66.6	68.9	1.6
2008	44.3	51.9	65.0	68.1	1.5
2012	38.0	49.5	63.4	69.7	1.8
2016	39.4	49.0	61.7	68.4	1.7

Source: Adapted from Wattenberg, 2016 p. 93; Modified by the author from US Census Bureau Surveys.

a jump from 15.9 percent turnout to 30.1 percent. That was nearly twice the jump by the 65+ age group which went from 57.5 percent turnout to 63.6 percent. Ordinarily that last number would have been extremely impressive, but it is minor compared to the younger age groups. The jump among the 18–24-year-olds actually moved their voting rates above that of the 25–44 age group in 2014. What is not clear at this point is whether the strong showing of youth is a harbinger of a renewed youthful engagement in electoral politics, or is it a product of a peculiar time in political history?

If we advocate that lowering the voting age can increase, rather than decrease youth voting rates, we should explain how our cure will fix the problem. Simply looking at Tables 4.1 and 4.2 can easily lead one to conclude that the 26th Amendment was a mistake. Instead of unleashing a mass of energetic voters upon the political status quo, it has generated an endless stream of lower turnouts by the youngest groups. And this has contributed to the overall decline in the US voting rates. But what explains this outcome rather than the forecast made by advocates in 1971?

To begin this, we shall look at the explanations that scholars have given regarding the underlying causes of this problem. The irony of the 26th Amendment is strong. It was implemented without being asked for, because society wished to atone for the wartime sacrifices society demanded of that generation. Yet, by giving them the vote at an inopportune age, they consigned them to a history of low voting. The irony is compounded since the young generation being rewarded was arguably the most politically engaged young generation in American history. That they were the generation to be responsible for lowering the US voting rates for decades is especially sad. It is

Table 4.2   Turnout by Age in Mid-Term Elections 1966–2018, in percentages

	18–24	25–44	45–64	65+	Ratio 65+: 18–24
1966	31.1	53.1	64.5	64.5	2.1
1970	30.4	51.9	64.2	57	1.9
1974	23.8	42.2	56.9	51.4	2.2
1978	23.5	43.1	58.5	55.9	2.4
1982	24.8	45.4	62.2	59.9	2.4
1986	21.9	41.4	58.7	60.9	2.8
1990	20.4	40.7	55.8	60.3	3.0
1994	20.1	39.4	56.7	61.3	3.0
1998	16.7	34.8	53.6	59.5	3.6
2002	17.2	34.1	53.1	61.0	3.5
2006	19.9	34.4	54.3	60.5	3.0
2010	19.6	32.2	51.1	58.9	3.0
2014	15.9	28.3	46.0	57.5	3.6
2018	30.1	40.4	55.0	63.8	2.1

Source: Adapted from Wattenberg, 2016 p. 109; Modified by the author from US Census Bureau Surveys.

important to note that whatever damage was done to the original Votes-at-18 generation has been passed along to succeeding generations.

The Amendment was followed by disappointing results in the 1972 election. That disappointing turnout turned out to be the highest score of the 18–24 since the voting age was dropped, which leads some to the logical question that if it did not work for this generation of 18–21, with their high education, fiery passion, engagement in politics—what in the world will result from going to a less politically educated, less passionate (subject to debate by the Parkland uprising, and the 2019 climate change demonstrations), and less politically engaged electorate? One skeptic argued that even if voting is habitual, why start where the odds are the worst?[6] That would, it was claimed, bring the habit of non-voting to another age group. In other words, we did enough damage to those earliest voters in the Votes at 18 era, so why would we want to do this to another cohort?

We will begin with the overall problem of low youthful voting rates, and then come back to the specific problems associated with the 26th Amendment. The explanations of low youth voting are many and varied, and for our purposes we can organize our analysis by grouping the explanations into three broad categories.[7] These can be called the Rational Choice, the Life-Cycle, and the Environment.

The first category of explanations for low youth voting rates comes from the rational choice category. This draws upon a deep and rich field of study into the reasons why anyone ever bothers to vote. For example, if young citizens do not feel as if elections matter, then putting time and energy into voting might not seem rational. However, this model does allow for individuals to decide that some elections are important enough or close enough to make going through the steps necessary to vote reasonable. Close elections might be a decreasing phenomenon as the country gets increasingly segregated into deeply red or deeply blue districts and states. Citizens in those situations could rationally decide that the outcome of the general election is not worth expending anything on. Thus, it can be argued that young citizens might rationally decide not to bother registering and voting. Rationally however, they should consider investing their time and energy into voting in the primary elections, but voting rates typically (though not in 2018) drop substantially in the non-presidential elections. For the most part, rationality claims help us understand why many voters, of whatever age or background, do not bother to vote.

Rational choice explanations are unable to explain convincingly why young people today find it less rational to vote than young people did 50 years ago, or why rationality is increasing among recent generations. We shall revisit this in the special case of young rational voters in the third category. By focusing on the rationality in cost-benefit terms we are ignoring non-rational reasons for voting (note: non-rational does not mean irrational). For example, citizens feel good participating in elections because it is a social exercise. Vote for the Blue Team! For the moment, at least, we will continue ignoring these motivations for voting.

A second category of explanations of low youth voting can be termed the life-cycle category. As cohorts age, their voting rates increase slowly, until old age takes over and voting rates for the cohort decline. Not surprisingly, the age at which old age begins to take its toll on voting rates, has moved upward as Americans have been living longer in good health. Highton and Wolfinger analyzed political life-cycles and asked whether it is assuming adult roles (marriage, career, home-owning, staying put, community ties, leaving home) that causes older citizens to vote at higher rates than younger voters. Naturally, there is a lot of overlap between these and their findings are not strong in supporting the thesis that adult roles are the key to increasing voting rates.

> Residential stability significantly facilitates turnout. Our multivariate analysis show that compared to people who have moved into their current residence within a year of election day, those who have stayed put for at least three years have a voting rate nearly eleven percentage points higher. Living in the same place for one to two years was worth about six points higher turnout.[8]

Their analysis of 18–24-year-olds showed that those attending college were 17 points higher than non-college students, and part-time college students were 11 points higher. Among the transitions they analyzed, only leaving school was significant and it was negative. "Students of all types are much more likely to vote than those who are not in school."[9] They concluded that when the entire set of adult transition factors are used to estimate the difference in turnout rates between someone with all these adult roles and someone who has none of them, it is only 5.9 percentage points, which they point out is far less than the 37-percentage point difference between the 18–24-year-olds and those in their 60s.[10] Thus, adult life transitions only marginally explain the age gap.

Moreover, this life-cycle phenomenon does not account for the decline in voting rates for the same age cohorts over time. Tables 4.1 and 4.2 show downward voting trends for three of the four age groups. Only the 65+ group does not show the same type of steady decline over the years. This group is growing larger as a percentage of the overall voting age population, and it is continuing to vote at its traditional high rates, and this ameliorates the decline in the voting rates of the younger cohorts. This effect may be attenuated as soon as the first generations of the 18-year-old voting cohorts are entering the 65+ age cohort. That time is fast approaching as an 18-year-old voter in the inaugural year of 1972 turned 65 in 2019. Since the 1972 cohort of 18-year-old voters voted at the highest rates of any 18-year-old voters, the decline in 65+ voting rates should begin to emerge over the next several election cycles as they are joined by lower voting cohorts.

These life-cycle arguments contend that young citizens are less integrated into society, they have less political knowledge, and they feel that they have less at stake in comparison to older voters. Related to this is that they typically have not established strong party loyalty, and they have certainly not developed the habit of voting. It is worth noting at this point that these are issues that every generation of citizens have confronted. This explains the higher turnout rates as age increases. But, since the voting rates have been dropping for the youngest voters as generations have passed, we must consider the possibility that changes in society are driving down the voting rates of contemporary young voters. On the other hand, we cannot reject out of hand the possibility that some recent social developments could increase youth voting, but there is not a lot of evidence of this thus far.

The third category (Environment) of explanations focuses on the social and media situations in which young generations are coming of age. These contend that the developments in technology have changed much in society, including our inclinations to see voting as an important civic act. Most of these arguments lament that younger generations are not embracing civic responsibilities at the same rate as prior generations. Charitable explanations point to the fragmentation of news sources and the exponential proliferation of entertainment options to citizens of all age, especially the young. These developments, which it is fair to say were not created by young generations, have robbed them of one or two shared sources of news, and have conspired to distract them from learning about and getting involved in politics and government.

Let us compare today's youth with those of the Truman and Eisenhower Administrations. Back then there were only a few choices of news sources and for the most part folks used the same sources as their neighbors. During much of the post–World War II era, the three big networks, ABC, CBS, and NBC, essentially mirrored each other in their approach to political news coverage. Politics and sports were the most commonly discussed matters. Today, as most readers will recognize, it is very different. Other scholars have reached similar conclusions explaining that the pattern of recent youth not-voting is based on rising living standards leading them to consider voting as just another right in a changing conception of good citizenship. Rimmerman established a hierarchy of political participation with three stages of activity. The bottom stage, which he called "spectator," includes, very prominently, voting. The second stage, which he called "transitory" includes going to public meetings and contacting officials. The third and highest stage, which he called "gladiatorial" includes raising money for candidates or becoming a candidate.[11] Although not all the high ladder activities center around young citizens, many do. It is worth noting that while there is inequality in the spectator act of voting, the inequalities tend to expand proportionally as one climbs the participation ladder described by Rimmerman.

The pace of media proliferation of entertainment which began with television, 8-track tapes, and dumb cell phones, did not really kick in until the second half of the 20th century. And the pace has not slowed down. The maturation of the web of course multiplied all these changes. Milner identified three stages of technological advances that have fundamentally changed the way we access information and communicate. He saw it beginning with the home computer, which evolved into the period of digitalization, followed by our current mode of high speed internet.[12] Moreover, this time-line conforms roughly to the accelerating decline of voting rates among 18–24-year-olds. More advanced technology means less voting by young citizens.

Ultimately, none of these three explanatory categories can, by themselves, provide a compelling explanation for the pattern of low voting shown in Tables 4.1 and 4.2, and thus they cannot guide us toward devising plausible solutions. By itself, the rational actor explanatory model can account for variations in voting based on the elections involved. Thus, close elections, or widely perceived important elections should generate higher voter percentages. But this is of little use when we seek to explain why young citizens are increasingly voting at low rates. For this we must shift the focus from the voters (and non-voters) to the nature of elections themselves. This allows us to still employ the rational actor explanatory model to explore these questions.

It can be difficult deciding between these theories and at the risk of violating Occam's Razor we can say that contemporary youth do not vote because they have less community investment, because they have many more options of news sources and of outlets for political expression, and as such it is rational for them to choose not to vote. Today's youth have exponentially more political information in their hands compared to earlier generations. At the same time, politics faces tough competition for their attention. Look! (Insert the name of some obscure to this author hip-hop artist) just dropped another song! This has expanded the range of not-voting justifications. Specifically, the fragmented news and proliferating entertainment options have robbed the political sphere of its pre-eminent place in the lives of citizens. Not long ago, politics and news along with sports dominated the newspapers. And newspapers are Martin Wattenberg's gold standard for gaining political knowledge. Even sports is finding its place in jeopardy—and the American sport of baseball faces entirely new sports competitors from around the world as they vie for loyal consumers.

If we begin with this formulation, we still need a way to know if our cure, or any cure, might modify the equation enough to raise voting rates. To untangle this, it may help to begin with the rational actor approach and consider all the elements that go into casting a vote in an election. By breaking this process down, which entails a variety of discrete steps, we can hope to identify points where changes can be made to generate more voting.

We cannot make voting rational, but we can make it more rational, or less rational. Some very smart people despair and move to advocating compulsory voting (Lipjhart and Wattenberg). We will not address this particular cure here, unless and until we also despair of all the other cures working. With that firmly in mind, let us approach the problem from another direction. Instead of focusing on voters/citizens, we turn our attention to the process of voting. This approach to understanding these voting gaps employs a framework that breaks the decisions and actions of voting into separate categories.

Elections are structured by rules and procedures to which citizens must conform if they wish to cast a legitimate ballot. Thus, elections prescribe who can vote, when they can vote, and where they can vote. All those rules and procedures by their very nature impose costs upon the citizen. These costs vary across the United States and across the democratic world. And they vary over time. Costs entail time, effort, and, sometimes, the monetary cost of completing the steps to voting. Governments change the rules and procedures periodically. In addition, and of great interest to us here, costs vary across individuals as well. So, for example one citizen lives within easy walking distance of the polling site, and another citizen lives two bus rides away. The first faces low costs in terms of getting to the polling booth while the second faces much higher costs.

Prospective voters vary in ways besides geography. They vary with respect to the resources that the individual brings to the decision of whether to undertake the steps required to cast a vote. What are these resources? Some very important resources are: political knowledge, prior experience in voting, and a sense of voting as an obligation.[13] Another source of resources comes from citizens feeling that they have a stake in the community. We might also consider distractions as things that could stand in the way of someone going through the steps involved with voting. Distractions are factors of life that can make voting seem less important. Among these are getting married, starting a new career, and moving to a new location. Finally, we can say that citizens vary in terms of having a habit of voting (or not voting). Habits of voting (or non-voting) are established like other habits after repeated experiences. Ultimately, habitual behaviors, including voting, become second-nature.

We are going to discuss costs/resources/distractions/habits (C-R-D-H) because these are very important with respect to new voters. We are discussing these because they have the largest impact on the newest voters, and these tend to be the youngest voters. We know that this group is more sensitive to variations on these than are older, more experienced voters.

PART TWO—COSTS

Voting is costly and non-voting, by contrast, is considered free. This is not always true because some citizens feel they are not fulfilling their civic duty when they miss voting in elections. But non-voting is also habitual. In fact, it is always easier to not vote than it is to vote. Costs are considered the activities a citizen must perform in order to cast a meaningful ballot. Every voting experience entails some cost. But what determines the impact of these costs?

A) Costs are highest at first election.
B) Costs drop with each successful election.
C) Moving and other factors can raise the costs of voting.
D) Fear of public humiliation. First-time voters fear their ability to cast proper voters. Sometimes the fear is technologically based. Sometimes the fear is that the voter has not done sufficient research on the candidates and issues. Professors go to the voting precinct and see friends and colleagues. New voters see sheriffs and judges and other imposing and highly educated and politically astute professionals.
E) Governments can raise or lower costs. One method governments have used to suppress voting turnout is to reduce the number, or move the location of polling booths. Research has confirmed that by extending the distance voters must travel in order to cast their votes, turnout rates are reduced.[14] Some of these costs were reduced by the 1993 National Voter Registration Act (also known as the Motor-Voter Act).

When examining costs, the process of becoming an eligible voter and casting a vote requires citizens to undertake actions that require them to expend things such as time, energy, and mental contemplation, though typically very little actual money. Costs begin with getting registered as a legally valid voter and culminates with walking out of the polling booth wearing both a smile and an I Voted sticker. Costs of course are not constant and vary across voting jurisdictions and are highly dependent on the previous experiences a citizen has with voting. Nonetheless, these costs when high, can lead citizens to sit out elections.

Costs vary from state to state just as the rules governing elections vary. Costs also vary over time for individuals. Having voted once or more reduces the costs of voting—not all steps, such as getting registered or learning where the polling booth is located, need to be replicated at each election. Costs may also rise—as, for example, when people age so that getting to the polling booth becomes more difficult.

As with other products, the costlier something is, the less it will be consumed. Thus, costly voting decreases the number of voters. Most proposed and recently implemented electoral reforms focus on reducing the costs of voting. Though the goal is to increase voting rates, the outcome is often the reverse.[15] For example, citizens in some states can vote by mail, and in many states voting days have been expanded under the name of early voting. In 1993 the federal National Voter Registration Act went into effect requiring states to offer voter registration when someone applies for a new or renewed driver's license. These efforts should push the voting rates up in the states that have implemented more of them in comparison to states without as many of these reforms.

John Holbein and D. Sunshine Hillygus surveyed the evidence regarding the impact of various electoral reforms on the magnitude of the youth vote and they found that some had negative or little impact, while a few had substantial positive results.[16] Among those reforms with negative impacts are early voting, election day registration, and no-excuse absentee voting. Among the reforms that are evidence of having positive impacts on the likelihood that young citizens will vote are online registration, preregistration, and same-day registration. They found that citizens 60+ did not show much of a response to these reforms. This underlines two important points. First is that registration complexities pose a real barrier to potential voters. Second is that these impacts appear much greater in the case of younger versus older voters.

This work is consistent with the work of other researchers who also have discovered that impacts of reforms will be felt more strongly among younger voters.[17] This is because older citizens have mostly developed in-grained habits of voting, or not voting, and they also have more resources. For them a little more convenience in the voting process is not very important. But for first- or second-time voters this might be consequential in determining whether someone bothers to vote or not. Consequently, the nature of elections determines youth voting rates much better than it explains the voting rates of older cohorts. This indicates that youth are more susceptible to barriers and to changes in electoral systems.

PART THREE—RESOURCES

Resources can be defined as the things that increase the likelihood that a particular citizen will vote. The sources of these qualities include families, schools, media, government, political actors, religion, and peers. Some of these resources are situated within the individual and some are situated in the social setting. In theory, all Americans can gain adequate political knowledge, internalize the sense of citizen obligations to vote, and develop an interest in politics.[18] Individuals are shaped by society and the social environment in which they are located. Some find government and politics dreadfully boring and abstract from their everyday lives.

In reality, individuals generate these characteristics in different measures. Individuals vary in terms of how many resources they bring to the voting decision process. Societies do not nurture the same resources in all its citizens. In many cases, minority groups are intentionally denied opportunities to build their resources. For example, the denial of basic educational opportunities blocks the ability to develop effective political knowledge.

Political knowledge is a very important resource. Eric Plutzer says, "Thus, political knowledge is a resource that can directly offset costs of initial turnout."[19] It is easier to decide to vote if you know something about what is on the ballot. And this is the primary role of education with special attention to civics courses. When citizens do not understand how the political processes work, voting can seem a pointless exercise. Indeed, it might seem like a distraction from the important things in life, like job and family. Empowered with political knowledge, citizens see elections in a different light.

There are other factors that vary from individual to individual that impact propensity to vote. Another important factor in building resources is the length of time someone lives in the same community. With time, the knowledge of local issues, and the commitment to the community rises and increases the chances the resident will vote. When the first election is in a new location, the odds of voting decrease. Moving decreases the odds of voting. Even if the costs of first-time voting are lowered (say by easing registration requirements) there will be higher costs for those without strong peer voting models.[20] As non-voters age, they gain political knowledge, appreciation of the impact of government policies, and thus they become more likely to vote.

Scholars have long identified the positive association of higher education and voting rates, but they have not agreed upon the mechanisms by which college generates this outcome. Kam and Palmer argue that college itself does not cause political participation, that things happen in the senior years of high school cause both participation and college.[21] Certain events can influence later voting habits, and these are termed period effects. Beyond these major events, things like parental characteristics, individual abilities, and predispositions play major roles. As Kam and Palmer state, "the literature on educational attainment points to systematic differences in who goes to college and who does not."[22]

Several scholars emphasize the importance of the social setting in which voting occurs.[23] Bhatti and Hansen emphasize the social aspect of voting with a focus on "who you live with."[24] So, when youth move from home they lose the positive impact of their (voting) parents, and gain the negative impact of their non-voting peers. This is consistent with the wide gap between 18+ who go to college and those who do not. In college, especially in recent years, the push for voting is very strong, and many peers are indeed voting.[25] Not so much for the non-college cohort.

The point is that the likelihood that someone will become a voter is shaped by forces and decisions happening prior to going to college. So, who someone lives with shapes the probability and the decision to go to college, and the same forces in turn shape them to become politically engaged. This is ameliorated even more by the choice of major that either increases or decreases the chances that a college student becomes a voter or not. There is also a self-selection effect in play, where students who are more likely to be voters are more likely to select majors like History, Political Science, and Sociology.[26] So, the hypothesis is that students tend to congregate with students in similar majors, so some groups will likely discuss politics a lot, and others rarely or only in derogatory and dismissive terms.

But these are examples of citizens with high levels of resources. Many citizens do not have these high levels. For them, the costs can be determinative whether they vote or not. The costs are therefore most important with respect to those citizens with low resources. This tends to be young and less-educated citizens. They often have few resources and have not developed the habit of voting and the experience of voting. These citizens can be mobilized at certain times and can be convinced to vote. At other times the mobilization efforts may not be as powerful and this group will include many non-voters.

The point here is that the choice made prior to college to not go to college, means that the young person is not inclined to become politically engaged, and will likely move into social circles that are young and also not inclined to become politically engaged, with very few voters. This is the hurdle that unions can help us overcome, but as they have gotten weaker and smaller that job is not being performed. When strong and numerous, the unions can mobilize workers and their families. In fact, the role of unions in encouraging voting is often undercounted because statistics often only include the union members themselves. In reality unions work to mobilize entire families (of eligible voters of course) and even neighborhoods to vote.[27] Their decline has been accompanied by the weakening of other civil society agents who have traditionally encouraged voting among their members.[28] In the United States and most Western democracies parties of labor are typically on the left side of the political spectrum. Their decline over the same time period that the voting age was set at 18 means that the left parties have experienced erosion of their base, with that base drifting into non-voters. To remain competitive the left parties have had to shift their focus to the educated elites who are socially liberal. This creates space for a politician with a populist appeal to excite and mobilize these forgotten folks.

Of course, the individual choices made to register and vote, or not to do one or the other, are not truly individual choices. They are always taken within a social context and the characteristics of the social context vary considerably over space and time. But, at any time there are actors that are interested in getting you to vote. Some of these are governmental entities, some are partisan political parties, and some are good government types, either organized into nonprofit actors, or random individuals who want to shape your behavior. Those who want you to vote will undertake mobilizing efforts to get you to register and get you to the voting booth. Those folks either want you to vote because it is good for the country, or because it is good for their side in the political battles. There are of course some who are trying to demobilize you, and who would prefer that you not vote. Each side in the political competition identifies what type of person is more likely to vote for them and who is less likely to vote for them. Naturally, they will try to mobilize the folks who are more likely to vote for them.

Mobilization efforts connect with our costs/resources/distraction/habit framework in several ways. Mobilization efforts are effective in reducing costs if and only if they help citizens get registered and to the polls. Mobilization can increase the resources a citizen has by nurturing the idea that voting is a citizen's duty and is an important communal act. Mobilization efforts also increase the political knowledge of citizens by providing information on the candidates, parties, and issues. Mobilization is often dedicated to reducing the distractions that citizens face. They do not try to eliminate the distractions, rather they work to make voting a higher priority than the other distractions. The roles mobilization plays become less necessary as the habit of voting develops.

These resources can be used to offset some of the costs of voting. Someone who believes a good citizen must vote, will overcome many obstacles to cast their vote. Martin Wattenberg recounts how his father, though very ill, demanded that his children transport him to the polling booth so that he could, once more, fulfil his duty as a citizen.[29] Someone who follows politics regularly, and did well in history and government classes will normally have a strong desire to exercise their vote.[30]

PART FOUR—DISTRACTIONS

Distractions are those things that do not raise the cost of voting, rather they decrease the likelihood of voting irrespective of the costs. In other words, Life. These distractions tend to diminish when a voting habit is formed.

However, they can interfere with habit formation at the front end. Recent generations face more distractions than previous generations. Thus, it is a pressing problem. Distractions are not typically the focus of political reforms as they are not usually connected to the election process. However, they can be directly connected as two examples will show. One is moving the voting date to a weekend when less people are working. Two is national daycare services that would free up parents to vote without deciding whether to take the children with them to the polling both. Many other examples could be imagined since distractions are plentiful, but only some of them would have direct connections to government policies.

The current minimum voting age of 18 is in the middle of a period of intense transitions. Thus, the distractions will be plentiful and many are very demanding upon the time and energy of those citizens. For example, moving toward marriage and parenthood, and moving away from home, starting a career, and paying bills are things that accelerate once someone graduates high school. And, all of them serve to distract the citizen from registering and getting otherwise prepared to vote. Many of these get easier over time (thus less distracting). Except, apparently, paying bills which for most of us remains quite distracting. An example would be a citizen expecting the birth of a child. Worrying about health considerations and financial issues along with myriad other concerns could easily distract a citizen from getting registered to vote and making it to the polling place on the right day. Critics of the 26th Amendment claim this is a big part of the problem of declining voting among young generations.

PART FIVE—HABITS

Habits develop over time and can be either habits of voting or of not-voting. Considerable research has confirmed that voting and non-voting are habitual activities. Mark Franklin employs terms such as "footprint" of the first election, and "young initiation" as the larger process by which youth are brought into voting.[31] This puts a focus on resources and maintains that life for 20–21-year-olds is a time of very low resources.

Voting becoming habit-forming is partly due to costs decreasing. These costs decrease because a registered voter does not need to re-register, knows where the polling booth is located, and is generally aware of the dates of the next election. We know that missing an election does not destroy the habit of voting. Conversely, a non-voter who is induced to participate in one election, is likely to continue as a voter in subsequent elections. Green and Shachar say, "Lure someone to the voting booth, and you will raise his or her propensity to vote in a future election."[32] Non-voting is a bad habit, as

Dinas maintains: "If voting patterns create some sort of path dependence, as the habit formation hypothesis suggests, then not voting when eligible may also leave a footprint on individuals' participation profiles. In other words, forming stable voting patterns may be more difficult if initial experience with political campaigns does not materialize into actual participation."[33]

Dinas points out that explanations for any particular choice to vote or not vote is often expressed in cost-benefit terms (thus it falls within the rational actor explanatory model).[34] However, research shows that over time, those calculations are less important and that habit having voted in election (1) makes it more likely to vote in election and (2) becomes more important as an explanatory variable. Eventually, the habit becomes a greater predictor of whether someone will vote in the next election, rather than race, age, economic status, or educational level of the citizen.[35] So, costs of voting, etc., are important in determining the first and second voting experiences, but less important as habits build.

Most non-voters transition into voters and then persist as voters.[36] As people get older their resources for voting (including knowledge) increase and if the costs of voting stay constant, then they are likely to switch from non-voting to voting. The reverse is not true, that voters who miss an election become non-voters, rather they return to their voting behavior. "As young citizens confront their first election, all the costs of voting are magnified: they have never gone through the process of registration, may not know the location of their polling place, and may not have yet developed an understanding of party difference and key issues. Moreover, their peer group consists almost entirely of other nonvoters: Their friends cannot assure them that voting has been easy, enjoyable, or satisfying."[37]

Wattenberg does not find evidence supporting the voting habit thesis in looking at the presidential elections of 2008–2012.[38] The 2008 election of Barack Obama caused 18–29-year-olds to vote at 8.7 percent higher rates than in 2004, and 30–44-year-olds to increase their vote by 4.4 percent. By contrast, the less than history-making election of 2012 saw a dip of 4.8 percent in 18–29-year-olds, and a smaller dip of 1.3 percent in 30–44-year-olds. He makes the mistake of expecting that young voters, inspired by Obama's first presidential election, would remain voters. He is disappointed because he is applying the rational actor model to individuals which is limited to explaining variations between elections depending on how close or important the elections are. He therefore misses the point of habits in that they do not form after one or two experiences. They do not take hold until a minimum of three or four elections have passed. Until then young citizens will be likely to switch to or from voting at a rate comparable to how often they change college majors. About 30 percent of college students change their major within their first 3 years of higher education, and 10 percent change their major at least twice during that period.[39] A 2018 survey of 18–24-year-olds indicated that a large percentage are politically undeclared. Only 56 percent affiliate themselves with either of the two major political parties. About a third described themselves as Independents.[40] Wattenberg reports that the 18–29 age group always supports third-party candidates in recent presidential elections at higher rates than any of the other age cohorts. These third-party candidates were George Wallace in 1968, John Anderson in 1980, Ross Perot in 1992, Ross Perot in 1996, and Ralph Nader in 2000.[41] Meanwhile older voters remain very stable in their partisan identification.[42]

Younger voters are more susceptible to factors that disrupt or complicate an election since they have not yet developed the habit. Following Franklin, Gallego says, "Just after leaving school or when attending university young adults are more likely to be in situations that are not conducive to learning to vote"—they are otherwise busy, don't have older role models to show them the ropes, and are unattached to locality.[43] The positive effects of staying in school and going to college hide the negative impact of having new adult roles and responsibilities. Added to this are the energetic efforts by several organizations to increase the rate of college student voting rates.[44]

PART SIX—INTERACTIONS

The way these concepts interact shapes the likelihood of voting-age eligible citizens to vote. First, we will discuss each in isolation and then in interactions with the others. Here are some guiding principles:

- Elections have costs
- Voters possess resources
- Voters face distractions
- When resources are greater than the costs and the distractions, the citizen will vote
- Voting adds to the resources a citizen has
- Citizens develop a habit of voting after 3–4 elections
- Once a habit is established costs become nearly inconsequential, so that a citizen with a voting habit will walk 15 miles (uphill both ways) in the snow to vote

In this section, we will argue that C-R-D-H represent variables that can be shaped if not determined by government policies and regulations. This leads then to a consideration of reforms that are possible and sensible. These in turn, make the circumstances at which voting/non-voting begins very important. Those factors are very important at First Election. When youth face First Election, the costs are magnified. Against these costs are resources that citizens have in varying amounts. These include political knowledge and sense of civic duty; sense of community; environmental factors such as peers or family who vote, etc. Resources are lowest at the youngest age. All of this implies that helping the first-time voter is the most important.

Moreover, newer voters are more susceptible to changes in costs than older and experienced voters. Raising the costs of voting will negatively affect the new voters more than experienced voters. Conversely, reducing the costs would predictably have a greater positive impact on newer voters than on experienced voters. The reason for this difference across ages is habit, not the characteristics of younger vs. older people. Much of the criticism of young citizens for their low voting rates overlooks the higher costs (coupled with fewer resources and no voting habits) facing Rookie Voters.

As a citizen moves from a first-time voter to a regular voter, costs go down, resources go up, distractions may or may not get worse, and habits grow stronger. Costs decrease with voting experiences. Having successfully navigated the voting process once means that the citizen will ordinarily be registered when the next comes around, and will know how to get to the polling booth. As costs go down, habits grow stronger. Reforms that lower costs make habits easier to form. Habits make the costs less consequential. When habits are ingrained, citizens follow the patterns they have already established. Ultimately, a regular voter will become oblivious to the costs and feel highly efficacious in the role of voter, and handles distractions easily, and thus becomes a *bona fide* habitual voter.

Young people attending college vote at higher rates than those who do not attend. Colleges help lower the costs for their students. The assistance usually comes with students setting up voter registration tables and the university putting voter registration forms and instructions in the physical mailboxes of residential students (required by federal law in 1965). Increasingly, colleges and universities have managed to bring polling booths to campus so that student voters need merely walk to a central location on campus. It is noteworthy that these services have not been offered to their former high school classmates who are not at college.

This discussion illustrates that the costs/resources/distractions/habits formula vary as a citizen evolves from a Rookie to a Veteran Voter. Young citizens, less-educated citizens, and poorer citizens are more vulnerable to that formula making voting irrational. For everyone their first election is special. The 10th election is still valuable but not as special as the first. The first election is important for non-voters as well. The negative footprint is left when a citizen neglects to register or vote.

CONCLUSION

This chapter began with the story of the 26th Amendment. In some ways, it is an inspiring story, especially for those of us who advocate for Votes at 16. However, the story does not end with passage of the 26th Amendment. Instead, it can be traced through time from when the 18-year-olds in 1972 graduate up to the 65+ age group in the 2020 elections. This part of the story reveals a steady decline in voting overall and in the 18–24 age cohort specifically.

The reason for this, it is claimed, is that it set the age at which the habit of voting should start at the worst of all possible times in the citizen's life-cycle. Consequently, generations have entered the eligible voting ages without developing the voting habit. And, if you are not developing the habit of voting, you are developing the habit of not voting.

So, the newly enfranchised 18–20-year-olds entered the electoral process low on the C-R-D-H scales. Many were away at war, or in college avoiding the war, or off to Philadelphia in pursuit of a great job and perfect lover. For them the costs of voting were high and sometimes extremely high. I cannot imagine how someone in South Vietnam could get an Absentee Ballot, though I trust this situation has improved. To their advantage, those with high school degrees had probably had two or three courses in American History, Civics, or Problems in Democracy. However, they would not be around old folks with regular voting habits. Most of their peers would be of their own age and unlikely to be voters. And, war, college, and Philadelphia all have plenty of distractions. Even the ones who stayed at home and got a job, probably had romantic aspirations and in general found their place in the adult world. Voting is not the easiest way to achieve either of these. And, finally, none of these first-generation voters could have any habit of voting. So, with the exception of strong political knowledge this age cohort was, and continues to be, high on costs, low on resources, high on distractions, and empty on habits of voting.

If 18 is the absolutely wrong age to begin the habit of voting, what makes 16 better? Why is dropping the voting age from 21 to 18 wrong, but dropping it from 18 to 16 right? The answer is found in the discussion of costs, resources, distractions, and habits. At 16, in comparison to 18, costs can be lowered, resources can be strengthened, distractions can be limited, and, consequently, habits can begin to build.

Today's youth have demonstrated, in a couple of high-profile examples, that they are full of politically engaged energy and can speak very passionately on political issues of the day and of the future. The eloquence of the Parkland School shooting survivors was heartbreaking but also inspiring. Their voices called out for the middle-aged and elderly lawmakers to take real action to protect schoolchildren, even if it risked their own political futures. The contrast was visible for all to see. Once again, it took the action of a bold young person, Greta Thunberg, to dramatize the confidence and determination of the youth in opposition to the national and international gridlocks on these important matters.

On the electoral stage the strong youth turnout in the 2018 elections confirmed that youthful political activism did not perish with the fading of the Baby Boomer generation. And, the two issues highlighted here seem likely to be with us for a long time. There is no reason to think that the era of mass shooting in our schools is behind us. And surely climate change will remain on the agenda of governments for years to come. The questions before us are these: Will the youth continue to rescue us from our folly and our inability to change the status quo? Is it folly to depend upon them to rescue us? Wouldn't it make more sense to inculcate them into full citizenship and voting early and hope they will vote often?

NOTES

1. Cultice. *Youth's Battle for the Ballot.*
2. Wattenberg. *Is Voting for Young People?*
3. Wattenberg. *Is Voting for Young People?*, 93.
4. Wattenberg. *Is Voting for Young People?*, 109.
5. Dottle, Rachael, Ella Koeze, and Julia Wolfe. "The 2018 Midterms, in 4 Charts." Political Analysis. *FiveThrityEight*, November 18, 2018. https://fivethirtyei ght.com/features/the-2018-midterms-in-4-charts/
6. Bergh. "Does Voting Rights Affect the Political," 90–100.
7. Fieldhouse, Edward, Mark Tranmer, and Andrew Russell. "Something about Young People or Something about Elections? Electoral Participation of Young People in Europe: Evidence from a Multilevel Analysis of the European Social Survey." *European Journal of Political Research* 46, no. 6 (October 2007): 797–822. https://ejpr.onlinelibrary.wiley.com/doi/full/10.1111/j.1475-6765.2007.00713.x.
8. Highton, Benjamin, and Raymond E. Wolfinger. "The First Seven Years of the Political Life Cycle." *American Journal of Political Science* 45, no. 1 (2001): 202–9. https://www.jstor.org/stable/2669367?seq=1#metadata_info_tab_contents, 205.
9. Highton and Wolfinger. "The First Seven Years," 207.
10. Highton and Wolfinger. "The First Seven Years," 202–9.
11. Rimmerman, Craig A. *The New Citizenship: Unconventional Politics, Activism, and Service.* Boulder, CO: Westview, 1998.
12. Milner. *The Internet Generation*, 58.
13. Foa and Mounk. "The Signs of Deconsolidation," 5–16.
14. Haspel, Moshe, and H. Gibbs Knotts. "Location, Location, Location: Precinct Placement and the Costs of Voting." *The Journal of Politics* 67, no. 2 (May 2005): 560–73. https://www.journals.uchicago.edu/doi/10.1111/j.1468-2508.2005.00329.x.

15. Burden, Barry C., David T. Canon, Kenneth R. Mayer, and Donald P. Moynihan. "Election Laws, Mobilization, and Turnout: The Unanticipated Consequences of Election Reform." *American Journal of Political Science* 58, no. 1 (September 9, 2013): 95–109. https://onlinelibrary.wiley.com/doi/full/10.1111/ajps.12063.

16. Holbein and Hillygus. *Making Young Voters*, 165.

17. Gallego. "Where Else Does Turnout Decline Come from?", 23–44.

18. McAvoy, Paula, Rebecca Fine, and Ann Herrera Ward. "State Standards Scratch the Surface of Learning about Political Parties and Ideology." Working Paper. ww.civicyouth.org: The Center for Information & Research on Civic Learning & Engagement, September 15, 2016. https://circle.tufts.edu/sites/default/files/2020-01/WP81_StateStandardsPoliticalIdeoloy_2016.pdf.

19. Plutzer, Eric. "Becoming a Habitual Voter: Inertia, Resources, and Growth in Young Adulthood." *American Political Science Review* 96, no. 1 (March 2002): 41–56. https://www.cambridge.org/core/journals/american-political-science-review/article/becoming-a-habitual-voter-inertia-resources-and-growth-in-young-adulthood/9EA1F561496D714346491B25B0D52239#.

20. Rakich, Nathaniel. "What Happened When 2.2 Million People Were Automatically Registered to Vote." Polling Organization. 538 Politics: Voting, October 10, 2019. https://fivethirtyeight.com/features/what-happened-when-2-2-milli on-people-were-automatically-registered-to-vote/?utm_source=pocket-newtab.

21. Kam, Cindy D., and Carl L. Palmer. "Reconsidering the Effects of Education on Political Participation." *Journal of Politics* 70, no. 3 (July 2008): 612–31.

22. Kam and Palmer. "Reconsidering the Effects of Education on Political Participation," 616.

23. Zeglovits and Zandonella. "Political Interest of Adolescents"; and Franklin, Mark N., Patrick Lyons, and Michael Marsh. "Generational Basis of Turnout Decline in Established Democracies." *Acta Politica* 39 (2004): 115–51. https://search.pro-quest.com/docview/217159473?pq-origsite=360link.

24. Bhatti and Hansen. "Leaving the Nest and the Social Act."

25. "Voter Friendly Campus." Education. Voter Friendly Campus, October 2019. https://www.voterfriendlycampus.org/; and "2018 Election Center." Education. CIRCLE. Accessed March 13, 2020. https://circle.tufts.edu/2018-election-center

26. Hillygus. "The Missing Link."

27. Freeman, Richard B. "What Do Unions Do.....To Voting?" Working Paper 9992. NBER Working Paper Series. National Bureau of Economic Research, September 2003. https://www.nber.org/papers/w9992, 3.

28. Commission on Youth Voting and Civic Knowledge. "All Together Now: Collaboration and Innovation for Youth Engagement." Equitable K-12 Civic Learning. Center for Information & Research on Civic Learning and Engagement, 2013. https://circle.tufts.edu/sites/default/files/2020-01/all_together_now_commi ssion_report_2013.pdf, 16.

29. Wattenberg. *Is Voting for Young People?*, 120–1.

30. Wattenberg. *Is Voting for Young People?*, 70–1; and Hillygus. "The Missing Link," 25–47.

31. Franklin, Lyons, and Marsh. "Generational Basis of Turnout Decline."

32. Green, Donald P., and Ron Schachar. "Habit Formation and Political Behaviour: Evidence of Consuetude in Voter Turnout." *British Journal of Political Science* 30, no. 4 (October 2000): 561–73. https://doi.org/10.1017/S0007123400 000247

33. Dinas, Elias. "The Formation of Voting Habits." *Journal of Elections, Public Opinion and Parties* 22, no. 4 (October 2012): 449. https://www.tandfonline.com/doi/ abs/10.1080/17457289.2012.718280

34. Dinas. "The Formation of Voting Habits," 431.

35. Dinas. "The Formation of Voting Habits," 449.

36. Plutzer. "Becoming a Habitual Voter."

37. Plutzer. "Becoming a Habitual Voter," 42.

38. Wattenberg. *Is Voting for Young People?*

39. U.S. Department of Education. "Beginning College Students Who Change Their Majors Within 3 Years of Enrollment." Data Point, December 2017. https://nc es.ed.gov/pubs2018/2018434.pdf.

40. "Young People's Ambivalent Relationship with Political Parties." Data Analysis. Center for Information & Research on Civic Learning and Engagement: Tufts University, October 24, 2018. https://circle.tufts.edu/latest-research/young-peo ples-ambivalent-relationship-political-parties.

41. Wattenberg. *Is Voting for Young People?*, 141.

42. Tucker, Patrick D., Jacob M. Montgomery, and Steven S. Smith. "Party Identification in the Age of Obama: Evidence on the Sources of Stability and Systematic Change in Party Identification from a Long-Term Panel Survey." *Political Research Quarterly* 72, no. 2 (2019): 309–28. https://journals.sagepub.com/doi/10 .1177/1065912918784215.

43. Gallego. "Where Else Does Turnout Decline Come from?" 27.

44. "Voter Friendly Campus."

Chapter 5

Getting It Done

The first four chapters have made an affirmative case for Votes at 16. Evidence from several countries and local elections where it has been implemented point to the conclusion that adding 16–17-year-olds to the voting rolls will not degrade our elections, that if anything, it should mark an improvement on the voting of the 18–21-year-olds. We surveyed two structural problems facing the American political system. These are the inequality of voting rates across several categories, most importantly across age and educational levels, and the overall low and declining voting rates in the United States. The argument was advanced that the declining voting rate problem originated in the decision, as noble as it sounded at the time, to drop the voting age from 21 to 18. This created problems because voting is a habitual activity and 18 is the wrong time to establish positive habits.

Now we shift gears and look at how this reform might gain approval and what might follow from the reform—what are its implications? This chapter takes up two challenges. First, it begins with a discussion of the potential manner in which this reform could come about. This analysis will utilize the historical record of successful (and one unsuccessful) efforts to enhance American democracy by adding new voters to the rolls. Second, the chapter will tackle the issue of civic education, which is central to the feasibility of the reform. The proposal places great emphasis on the role of civic education courses in the secondary education curriculum in public schools.

These two topics are connected because one without the other will have limited positive impact. If we just have Votes at 16 without any reform to civic education, we will expect to see limited improvement in youth turnout and some development of habitual voting behavior. If we reform civic education (aka active civics) without instituting Votes at 16, the lessons in civics will remain abstract and probably boring to most students. The complementary nature of these two reforms is clear in the empirical accounts of Votes at 16 that we discussed in chapter 1. But what is not clear is whether one should precede the other and if so, which one should be instituted first. One could argue that having active civics in place before Votes at 16 would make Votes at 16 perfect at the outset. On the other hand, one could argue that Votes at 16 would be a powerful driver of reforms toward active civics. But that debate is not our concern here.

PART ONE—HOW MIGHT IT HAPPEN?—3 MODELS

A recent study discussed the way debates over expanding the electorate by instituting Votes at 16 were waged in several different countries.[1] Most of the examples are drawn from the United Kingdom but are useful for other political contexts as well. The authors identified four models that characterize these varying approaches. Briefly they are categorized as (1) Good for kids; (2) Good for society; (3) Good for political party; and (4) Status quo is bad for kids. The first represents arguments based on the impact of the proposed reform on the political socialization of youth if they can begin voting at 16. It emphasizes the importance of very early positive political interactions on their future political development. The second, which the authors call their social capital model, emphasizes the benefits of bringing new and energetic voters into the fold and alleviating some of the malaise that surrounds politics in many Western democracies.[2] The third model is termed valence politics and refers to the calculations political parties make about the impact of supporting or opposing Votes at 16. In general, there is compelling evidence that parties of the Left, including environmentally focused parties, expect the most political benefit from the new voters. Generally, the Left parties push for Votes at 16 in the countries that have adopted it. Their final model is called political incentivization. This emphasizes the negative impacts of leaving these young citizens outside of full citizenship. Young people have awareness of the political environment around them through their phones and other modes of social media. Many of them see the political system as dysfunctional and unappetizing. If nothing is done to bring these youth into the political system, they are likely to never become politically engaged.

These arguments can be collapsed into a single coherent phrase—Left political parties support Votes at 16 which will benefit the society in the long run, and in the short run it will counteract the tendency toward youthful disengagement and nurture the positive political socialization of young people. Note of caution: Whenever you hear something that is able to solve many separate problems, be very skeptical. For example, if you see an ad for a potion that will brighten your smile, improve your memory, and make you an irresistible lover, only buy limited amounts. It is possible that the power of the positive goals cloud the reasoning processes.

When considering how a reform that proposes to expand the electorate might gain approval, we can imagine that if two arguments could be made eloquently and persuasively, all would be good. The first argument would be that the reform is good for ones being brought into the electorate. The second argument would be that the reform is good for society writ large. If it is good for the group, and for society, who could oppose it? Politicians and political parties, that is who!

We will proceed from here by looking at how these three factors might play out in the case of Votes at 16. We will make use of the historical examples of earlier expansions of the electorate, and we will discuss one proposed amendment that did not gain approval despite the many signs that pointed toward its easy passage. That failure is the Equal Rights Amendment (ERA). Note that the ERA would not expand the electorate in any direct fashion. It is being used in this discussion as a model of a major reform that everyone expected to get adopted but ultimately failed.

The 15th Amendment (1870) was a case of society doing the right thing and rewarding African American men for the service that many of them provided to the Union military cause during the Civil War. It was conceived that this change would perhaps have a providential impact upon the African Americans themselves, but there was little discussion of the positive impact this could have on society broadly speaking. During the debates of that time, efforts were made to reassure anxious White Americans that extending suffrage to African American men was just for voting purposes and not to integrate them fully into American society.[3] On the political front, with the Republican Party controlling the federal government, the discredited Democratic Party was unable to block the Amendment.

The 19th Amendment (1920) was targeted mostly for the benefit of women who had originally been totally excluded from voting, and mostly excluded from the political sphere. Moreover, it was narrowly tailored to not claim to bring women total equality within American society, but rather only to allow women equal voting rights. This process started and proceeded by working through the states first, thereby building pressure on the national government. As states, especially big states, extended the voting rights to women, more and more politicians recognized the tide of history, and fewer and fewer politicians considered it wise to cast a vote against a group that would soon constitute a half or more of the electorate. Ultimately, a majority of Republicans and a minority of Democrats combined to pass the Amendment through Congress and opened the way for state ratification to follow.

Civil Rights legislation in the 1960s was pushed forward by mass mobilizations and challenges to the prevailing Jim Crow status quo. Without those heroic efforts, the American South might not have changed yet. The history is rich with a combination of court challenges, political maneuvering, and popular agitation.[4] The ubiquity of television sets and a limited number of channels all nearly showing the same video clips brought the brutality of the Jim Crow south to viewers who had never ventured below the Mason-Dixon Line. Dr. Martin Luther King Jr. effectively connected the civil rights movement to the nation's founding documents by appealing to the Declaration of Independence and the Constitution. The immediate impact of the passage of the 1965 Voting Rights Act is clearly visible in the African American registration in Mississippi which increased from 6.7 percent registered voters in 1965 to 59.8 percent in 1967.[5] This led to a deep fissure within the Democratic Party. Northern Democrats were in favor of the laws. But southern Democrats were steadfastly opposed. This opened up the south to Republican candidates in the future.

The 26th Amendment (1971) instituting Votes at 18 was seen as a righteous and wise move at the time. The young people themselves would benefit as they would have the power to vote on the politicians who were making decisions about the war in Vietnam. Society would reap the rewards from a highly energetic and motivated phalanx of young people marching into the voting booths and town hall meetings across the country. Those youth, inspired by charismatic and idealistic leaders like Martin Luther King Jr., John Kennedy, and Robert Kennedy, would bring forward a liberal and egalitarian America. (Parenthetically and sadly, before the 26th Amendment was adopted, those three inspirational leaders were each assassinated, robbing that youthful generation of their role models, but they nonetheless voted at higher levels than any succeeding cohort of 18–24-year-olds.) In 1970, Congress passed the Voting Rights Act Amendments of 1970, which would have dropped the minimum voting age to 18. But states appealed the legislation to the Supreme Court where a 5–4 majority voided it for trampling on the rights of states to set their own voting rules. This decision was consistent with the Constitutional decision to allow states to determine voting rights. This caused the backers to go the Constitutional Amendment route and it was completed in near record time. As we saw in chapter 4 it is often portrayed in hindsight as a mistake.

The Equal Rights Amendment had been championed by every president for the past 50 years when it was passed by both houses of Congress in 1972, but still was not ratified because the necessary three-quarters of the states never voted in favor of its ratification. While efforts were made to broaden the appeal by advancing the claim that society on the whole would benefit, not just women, it was difficult to avoid the perception that it was only a benefit to women.[6] Any promise to improve the position of women in society, by its very nature, promises to change society. The history of the ERA shows it received fast and overwhelming support and was well on its way to a quick ratification. The positive aspects seemed self-evident. Women were clearly intelligent, capable, and experienced. Congress approved the Amendment by wide margins in both houses, winning strong majorities in both parties. The tide abruptly reversed direction when its opponents successfully switched the debate from the benefits to women, to the changes they feared it would cause in society. For example, would the next military draft have to include females alongside the males? Would they have to share the same foxholes? Would the ERA dramatically upend traditional male-female relations in all realms, from the boardroom to the bedroom to the battlefield?

Looking over these cases a few points deserve discussion. In terms of framing the issue, there seems to be more success when the focus is on the excluded group, with the ERA being an example of where a sure thing was defeated when it was portrayed as likely to fundamentally transform the entire social structure. The 26th Amendment comes closest to this end of the spectrum because its champions did highlight the benefits that would accrue to society with its passage. But the main focus of discussions was that the soldiers being sent to fight our wars deserved no less than all of the rights of full citizenship, including voting.[7] The passage of the Civil Rights legislation in the mid-1960s was accompanied by images of brutality against peaceful protestors, including children, and by calls by King and others for America to live up to its ideals. By contrast, the 15th and 19th Amendments were advanced without any promises of integrating the excluded groups fully into political society. Instead, advocates insisted that voting and only voting was the purpose of the amendments. The political cases in each of the scenarios are so different that it is difficult to identify any particular lessons.

Which model would apply to the case of the 16–17-year-olds? Society, simply deciding to extend the vote to the 16-year-olds because it is right, is unlikely to repeat what happened with dropping the voting age to 18. Though the American political system certainly has its share of dysfunction and complaints, rarely do voices call for bringing 16–17-year-olds into the political arena to fix it. The tide may be shifting as folks under the age of 18 are making their way into prominent media stories—with the coverage being generally positive (and of course not without virulent detractors). Beginning with the Parkland High School shooting aftermath, the extraordinary eloquence and passion of the surviving classmates stood in stark contrast to the middle-aged and very-aged politicians of both parties who seemed only temporarily interested and totally incapable of devising effective solutions. Nevertheless, the March for Our Lives movement is unlikely to sustain the energy necessary to effect such a major political change.[8] If the momentum continues it will likely be propelled by youth who are of voting age. A fundamental problem with youth is that they graduate, literally, to other things and interests. Thus, the movement is constantly losing its best and most experienced leaders.

Nonetheless, the prominent 16–17-year-olds who have made waves in the public media have not emphasized lowering the voting age. In Russell Dalton's engaged citizen model, they are mostly engaging in politics through direct action, rather than through the established electoral and legislative processes. They, once again in accordance with Dalton's model, were mobilized around one particular issue. This is distinct from earlier generations of young radicals (see Students for a Democratic Society, established in 1962) which came into politics with ideological perspectives they applied to a wide range of issues.[9]

Not only are the elders unlikely to advocate for extending the vote downward—they are likely to resist it vigorously. In recent decades, going back to the 1970s after the voting age was dropped to 18, young people have been criticized for their lack of political knowledge, limited political interest, and sporadic political participation. These complaints have grown stronger over time. In the words of one contemporary author, this generation is the "Dumbest Generation."[10] Millennials (born during 1980–1996) have been chastised for not stepping up to the political plate even as they prepare to replace Baby Boomers as the largest generation in the electorate. From this perspective, opening voting to the 16–17-year-olds seems like a recipe for the further degradation of American democracy.

Google searches easily deliver several websites and articles dedicated to advancing the cause of lowering the voting age. Some influential elites in the scholarly world have picked up this cause in books and articles. Scholars, such as Mark Franklin, Henry Milner, Daniel Hart, and James Youniss, have embraced or at least expressed openness to the idea. However, this does not yet comprise a wave of support among educated elites. And this is far from making progress in the thinking of the general public. A survey conducted in the United Kingdom found support ranging between 26 percent and 34 percent depending on how the question was asked.[11] Currently there are no national surveys in the United States of the wisdom of allowing 16-year-olds to vote.

Earlier expansions of the electorate via constitutional amendments had the virtue of advocating for human beings who were as mature as the preexisting electorate. The 16-year-old voting proposals have the misfortune of advocating for clearly lesser (because younger, and they will become full-fledged in time) citizens getting the right to vote. It is true of course that opponents of the earlier suffrage expansions denied that those proposed new voters were their mental equals. At this time the argument is not (or should not be) that 16–17-year-olds are as politically wise and sophisticated as the rest of us, but rather that they are wise and sophisticated enough. Even this will not satisfy everyone. Thus, we will continue to explore the other benefits to lowering the voting age.

From this discussion, it appears that chatter in the public realm emphasizes the injustice of denying the vote to this category of citizens. The focus tends to be on how 16–17-year-olds pay taxes, yet they cannot vote. Nonetheless, we are currently far from the society agreeing that there is any kind of injustice. Another point that has not gotten much traction is that by opening the voting to that age group we will be providing them with a richer political socialization experience and this will translate to enhanced political engagement though adulthood. Each of these arguments amount to the little-j justice concept. The key to Big-J Justice is to connect what benefits the group to the overall well-being of the society.

We have seen how the 26th Amendment was justified in part by its promise of injecting new and energetic (and thankful) voters into the troubled political system. Thus, it seems like pitching the reform as a solution to injustice to a small group will not prevail, which suggests that shifting to the benefits to society is the better strategy. At this point governmental officials are not feeling any pressure from the society demanding something be done, which means that the chances are that intellectuals and opinion leaders will play a major role in generating moral pressure on the elected officials. To make this argument for Votes at 16 will require more best-selling books (like this one is sure to be). Instead of a presidential candidate whose poll numbers rarely got above 3 percent being the most prominent advocate, someone with a higher profile is needed, perhaps Oprah? What will their main argument be? That this reform will make our elections more representative of the country and begin to push up voting rates, and do all the other little-j justice stuff.

Whichever model applies, the question of the mechanics of approval remains to be answered. The following considerations must be taken into account. First, the federal nature of our constitutional amendment process and our election laws means there are two potential paths forward. One starts in Congress, the other starts in one or more of the states. Second are the questions of who would champion the reform and who would oppose it. Of course, we also want to know the reasons for each. Third, taking this another step forward, we want to explore the reasoning for individual politicians and political parties to adopt a favorable or unfavorable position on this reform.

Broadly speaking, two paths are available. Technically, a third path, which involves a convention of the states. That has never been called and does not enter into any realistic calculations. The first path is via Congressional adoption first. Congress must pass the Amendment by two-thirds majorities in both Houses. If this is accomplished, it will be sent to the states where three-quarters are required to ratify. The second path is technically separate from the formal amendment process because it begins with state adoption of the lower voting age. The state-by-state approach could make very slow progress, especially if it begins with a non-prominent state (my desire to sell books across the country prevents me from identifying who that might be). If on the other hand, a very prominent state (California, New York, or Texas) began the adoption process, there would be strong pressure for other states to follow.

The choice between the two paths could depend on which is perceived the easiest to accomplish, and it is too early to guess which it will be at this juncture. State adoption has the advantage of allowing advocates (and opponents) to concentrate their resources rather than expending them at the national level. Operating at the Congressional level has the advantage of generating a great deal of free airtime that can reach the masses across the country even as the events play out in Washington, D.C.

Now, we can address the question of who, in general, will support, and who will oppose the reform. And how politicians and parties will calculate whether to support or oppose and risk the wrath of future voters remembering and punishing that vote in the ballot box. Unlike earlier expansions, where African Americans were not eventually going to become White, and women were not eventually going to become men, the 16–17-year-olds will become 18 and will be able to remember who voted Yea and who voted Nay on their voting rights.

Whether dropping the voting age to 16 to build the habit of voting will change the fortunes of the Left parties is an open question. In the United States this is the Democratic Party. There is reason to believe it could help since young people tend to be more liberal than older folks. This more liberal orientation of young people might be temporary, at least in its strength. Moreover, there is some evidence that high school graduates, who are also young, tend to tilt toward the conservative side.[12]

Politicians in democracies have a variety of goals. Some are deeply personal, and some are grandly for the common good. But, most of them are predicated on winning elections. Since incumbents are naturally conservative in the sense of resisting change to their constituencies since they know how to win with the existing constituency, they will need to be convinced that a newly configured electorate positively affects their future chances.

The chances of victory are connected to the likely voting age population in the voting district. Whatever the qualities of the politician—each will prefer some electorates to others. A successful politician is one that can win an election—and an incumbent is a successful politician. The incumbent has won with an existing electorate and would probably accept running for re-election in the same electorate. But, as poets and philosophers tell us, you cannot actually run in the same electorate two years later. There will be deaths, people moving in, people moving out, and new voters becoming eligible.

In other words, a politician cannot draw from the same voting pool twice. Naturally, he/she likes the current electorate and will seek to protect it. There are, of course, ways that any electorate might be improved—areas in which the opponent did well can be moved into another jurisdiction, or favorable voters in an adjoining district can be brought into the electorate. Conversely, districts can be made worse. One's own supporters can be moved out, for example. At its worst, these impulses culminate in politicians selecting their voters.

Politicians vary in their self-confidence but few incumbents would welcome a proposal to fundamentally transform their electorate. Like normal humans, politicians tend to be risk-averse. That is, they are more worried about losing than they are optimistic about winning. Imagine an incumbent politician who is given a choice between Electorate A, which is pretty much the one he/she was elected in, and Electorate B, whose mix of voters is completely undefined. Electorate B would as likely be better as it would be worse than Electorate A. Being risk-averse, the incumbent would be inclined to pass on the wild card (Electorate B) and stick with the status quo (Electorate A). Thus, even though coming out better off, electorally speaking, is a coin-toss, few incumbents would likely rush to choose Electorate B. Conversely, the politician or party that lost the last election might well gamble on what's behind Door #2 and consent to a fundamental transformation of the electorate.

In fact, with a few bits of critical information added to the description of Electorate B, the likelihood of an incumbent politician accepting the alternative Electorate will move from a coin toss to a high probability in one direction or the other. The bits of information would include data about the composition of the constituency regarding race, class, age, and perhaps percentage of college graduates. With that additional information, the politicians could make an informed decision.

Of course, the decision will be shaped by other factors, most directly by the margin of victory in the previous election. If the margin is small, the politician might rationally be more likely to roll the dice on a new electorate. If the margin is large, the politician will require a great deal of persuasion to give up their safe seat. Of the 19 House of Representatives members who voted against the 26th Amendment, 17 were from very safe seats (earning 60%+ of votes in the 1970 election) and 12 were Republicans. Two either did not run again or were defeated in their primary in 1972. Only five incumbents saw their winning percentages increase from 1970 to 1972. With House incumbents winning at a 94 percent clip, it is not surprising that the vote did not cause electoral defeats.[13] In addition to coming from overwhelmingly safe seats, these 19 could have felt safe risking taking an unpopular position, because they would only face the potential anger of three years' worth of voters (18-, 19-, and 20-year-olds). This can also be a factor when Votes at 16 reaches the same point because only two years' worth of voters are involved (16–17-year-olds).

Few voters would be likely to vote against candidates due to their vote on the proposal if the proposal fails. However, if the proposal succeeds and is put into practice, the newly enfranchised young voters are likely to reward/ punish elected officials for their stand on the reform. Older voters might have opinions, even strong ones, on the reform, but most would not have that as a deciding factor when going to the polls. Younger voters might, however, be quite motivated, as this reform would be the biggest political issue in their universe.

Incumbents will need to be reassured that any change or reform being proposed does not jeopardize their chance to serve the citizens once more. And it is incumbents who will decide on this particular reform. So, what can we say to these folks? First, we can reassure them that the new voters will represent only a small portion of the total electorate in the next election. There are no known geographic areas with a relatively high concentration of 16–17-year-olds. In other words, since 16–17-year-olds are mostly living in family households, their voting impact will be diluted by all the older people with whom they live.

Second, we will reassure them that the new voters are probably very similar to the rest of the electorate in their political orientation. They will be especially comparable to the 18–21-year-olds. Thus, they are no more likely to vote for the opponent than anyone else. In fact, the incumbent should seek to solidify the future support of the new voters by endorsing, not opposing, their enfranchisement. It is nearly always safer to be on the right side of history.

However, there is a distinction between the older citizenry and the 16–17-year-olds (and younger) in terms of race. The 16–17-year-olds are much more diverse racially and ethnically than older cohorts. For instance, the White population dropped from 62 percent to 51 percent in the period from 2000 to 2017. The African American population dropped slightly from 15 percent to 14 percent, with the Hispanic population growing from 16 percent to 25 percent and Asian population growing from 3 percent to 5 percent.[14] The impact of this is multiplied by the fact that this changing demographic is not temporary. Rather it will work its way through the population, and eventually restructure the electorate.[15] In this sense running away from 16–17-year-olds due to their demographic composition is ultimately a losing strategy.

Individual politicians should not look much past the next election, whereas the party can look a few elections forward. Anything longer risks making major mistakes. Political parties' policy preferences can change over time, and the world and the political landscape is almost, certainly, going to change. So, even when risk aversion prevails, the old formula might not continue to yield successes.

We can think of politicians as individuals, or in groups known as political parties. Aggregating the interests of individuals will invariably generate situations where the interest of the party diverges from the interest of individuals. Beyond incumbents, both major political parties are of course interested in their long-term viability and the impact of any potential political reform on their prospects.[16] What unites the individual politician and his party is the goal of winning elections. Typically, the party benefits when the individual party member wins.

From the perspective of the political party things look a little bit different. Parties, in comparison to individual politicians, tend to view proposed reforms from a slightly broader and longer frame perspective. Bold party leaders might embrace a reform that could reshuffle the deck in the near term in districts that typically or recently have had close elections. They might endorse the reform, if they feel that it would advantage them in the longer term. In this sense, the party would be choosing to be on the right side of history.

Efforts to restrict voting of college-age students are only feasible because in many cases the 18-year-olds in college live together in concentrated areas, i.e., college towns. If the Republican Party fears that college students are predominately liberal it is relatively easy to isolate a campus to make voting more difficult. On the other hand, if Democrats are worried about the perceived conservatism of non-college students, their dispersal throughout the population makes it infeasible to target them to keep them from voting.

This section covered the strategies and choices surrounding gaining approval for this reform. What type of argument is going to be most effective in persuading skeptics? Is it going to be to emphasize the injustice done to these young taxpayers? Or, is it going to be to emphasize how desperately society needs what these young people have in abundance: energy, imagination, and dedication to making the world a better place? Once public or elite opinions begin to swing in the direction of Votes at 16, what political approach will be wisest? Would it be beginning in the states and hoping that momentum will build and ultimately pressure the Congress to take up the issue? Or would it be focusing on the national political stage and seek to convince the Congressmen and Congresswomen and Senators to support the reform? Finally, what would incumbents and political parties do when they face this issue? Incumbents are likely to be reluctant to change, but some might see it safer to support the reform if the tide of history seems to be pushing for approval. Political parties would be able to take a longer view of matters, and probably the Democratic Party would be the first to embrace the amendment. If the Democrats lead the way, will the Republicans be able to resist joining? They would be able to stop the momentum with their numbers in Congress, but they would risk having their opposition limit their support with upcoming generations of voters. The Democrats would surely seek to take advantage and appeal to the young voters.

PART TWO—ACTIVE CIVICS

Civic education has been constantly praised by political leaders and educators as key to keeping American democracy vibrant. Folk wisdom identifies knowledge of the principles and institutions of our political system as essential to inculcating democratic norms into new generations and immigrants. That democracies need to have citizens who understand the basic institutional features of their political system, is a nice thought, and in an ideal world, this would be the normal condition of things.

We seem to believe in civic education, but deep analyses indicate it may be of limited effectiveness. The story of civic education is full of disappointing evaluations. Unfortunately, the positive impact of civics has been difficult to certify. Civics courses are designed to raise the scores citizens receive on political knowledge surveys. By many measures civic knowledge has not improved over the last 50 years even though education levels have risen considerably. Civics classes are generally considered to also be of limited value in increasing the political skills and values of high school students. In the stark estimation of one group of prominent education scholars, "taken as a whole, the nation's current civic education efforts are insufficient."[17] And, as we have seen already, there are grave concerns regarding the degree to which contemporary youth subscribe to basic democratic precepts.

Contextually, the world's largest democracy, India, has very low literacy rates (around 70%). We presume that not many Indians have read their version of the Federalist papers. Meanwhile, the worlds' oldest democracy, the United States, has demonstrated in survey after survey that citizens know very little about our political system.[18] This situation is exacerbated by the state and federal governments shifting funding and attention away from civics and toward the language arts and STEM subjects. As Hart and Youniss point out, until the 1960s, most public schools had three required courses for these purposes: 1) American History; 2) Civics; and 3) Problems in Democracy. Now those are combined in some fashion into one course.[19] Jamison contends that civics courses are constrained from fulfilling their missions by the supremacy of STEM in legislators' educational priorities, inadequate textbooks, and perhaps most daunting of all, fear of teaching politics in a bitterly partisan environment.[20]

By some measures the civics movement is alive and well.[21] For instance, all 50 states require some sort of American Government; American History; or Civics course before graduation.[22] Most of them, but not all, require that students pass the course. Moreover, there are 12 states that have adopted passage of a citizenship exam as a graduation requirement.[23]

As a consequence of survey results continually demonstrating a lack of political knowledge among American citizens, and in the context of our decentralized educational system, many new approaches have been championed to fix the problem.[24] At least three general approaches can be identified. One is modeled on Thomas Dewey's notion of modeling democratic practices in the classroom. A second seeks to promote democratic virtues by taking students into their communities, and engage in some service learning experiences. A third emphasizes standard political knowledge in the form of Constitutional principles and the historical evolution of our political institutions. Because the United States has traditionally left most of the curricular and funding decisions and powers to the states, and they to the local school districts, there has been, and continue to be, a mix of these approaches across the country.[25] However, the third is by far the easiest to assess by standardized testing and is the most widespread variant.

There has been very limited evidence that what is learned stays with the individual after graduation. For example, a civics education program titled Student Voices had students identify and define the problems in their community to be analyzed, with faculty serving as guides.[26] Among other results, researchers found that students who went through that program voted at higher rates than comparable students who did not go through the program. Lots of other imaginative approaches have been implemented. Fortunately, there are several civics scholars with alternatives to existing civics requirements and they have generated a list of recommendations.[27] Among these are broad proposals to involve families in design and delivery of the civics curriculum. Administrators should support teachers and encourage collaboration to foster innovation which they can then assess for effectiveness and improvement. Holbein and Hillygus decry what they describe as "bubble sheet civics."[28] This is their term for civics that emphasizes facts and numbers rather than emphasizing some of the non-cognitive aspects of becoming a full citizen. They claim that while there is some evidence that students are learning some facts, there is no evidence that the students are more likely to become voters or otherwise engaged citizens. They contend that young people want to become voters but only about half of those wind up voting. Life gets in the way. Holbein and Hillygus want civics classes to help with the practical sides of being citizens, and that includes the mechanics of registering and voting. In other words, active civics supports Votes at 16.

Hart and Youniss advocate for a focused engagement with a topic that has energized young people at least from the time of the original Earth Day in 1970, when your author and classmates went outside of our rural school building to demonstrate our appreciation of nature, to the sailing across the Atlantic by Greta Thurnberg in 2019. The choice of the environment seems ideally suited for such an approach since urban, suburban, small town, and rural environments all face challenges. Furthermore, the environment touches on virtually every other subject matter taught in schools: science; politics; culture; economics; literature; and health. As they acknowledge, one problem is that education budgetary allocations for civics are limited and under continued pressure.

Currently, there is a movement among states to make high school graduation contingent upon students passing a citizenship exam comprised of questions taken from real tests that aspiring naturalized American citizens must pass.[29] Recall that Purdue University is considering requiring a similar graduation requirement for their undergraduates because of the concern that many are graduating without sufficient political knowledge.[30] One should appreciate the irony of this. One of the original roles of public schools in the United States was to facilitate the integration of immigrant children into mainstream American culture, including into the political culture. Now, we are recognizing that our high school and even our college graduates are unlikely to pass a citizenship test.

In 2016 the Center for Information & Research on Civic Learning and Engagement (CIRCLE) reported on the status of state standards for teaching about political parties and political ideologies.[31] Their position was that civics should go beyond providing students with enough background information to formulate opinions. This is laudable but not sufficient. Instead, they argue, students should be able to place their opinions in the context of the political parties and ideologies that dominate American democracy. At even a higher level of understanding, they believe that students should be able to connect their own position in terms of both political partisanship and political ideologies. This would entail exploring the ideological underpinnings of the major political parties, rather than relying just on their gut instincts. They fully recognize that this is a tough task in the context of our highly polarized political culture.

They surveyed all 50 state civics education standards to see if they refer to: political parties; political ideology; issues and platforms; and how the student's belief fits into the ideological and partisan landscape. Their results are mixed. They report that 43 out of 50 state standards do mention political parties, but only eight mention political ideology. Not surprisingly, only ten (20%) states mention discussing political issues and platforms. It is not surprising that the number is so low, because of the contentious partisan polarization. But it is disappointing if the goal is to prepare young people to be fully engaged and well-informed citizens. On the ultimate preference of the CIRCLE researchers, only one state out of 50 mentioned that students should be able to connect their own beliefs into the larger societal landscape of political parties and ideologies. They discovered that when ideology is discussed it is generally done using the past tense, in history standards. The scholars chose the North Carolina standard as the best of the eight states that included explicit references to ideology:

> Analyze America's two-party system in terms of the political and economic views that led to its emergence and the role that political parties play in American politics (e.g., Democrat, Republican, promotion of civic responsibility, Federalists, Anti-Federalists, influence of their parties, precincts, "the political spectrum," straight ticket, canvass planks, platform etc.).[32]

At the same time, one suspects that many of these required courses are being taught by jaded teachers who dread discussing constitutional principles with disinterested youth who find the 1700s less interesting than . . . just about anything else on social media. Political issues and political platforms are the things that are generally considered to be relevant to new voters. It is fine to appreciate the Founding Fathers and the Federalist Papers, but typically young learners want to learn more about the debate about the current military intervention, or the next election. One reason that civics courses are boring to students is that even if most of the discussions are about citizens and citizenship, their full citizenship, including very prominently, voting, is two or more years away. That is a long time (1/8 of a 16-year-old's life) to wait. Not to mention that the Federalist Papers were written a very long time ago. Moreover, by the time that students become eligible to vote, all the news and most of the burning issues of the day will be different. Why should a rational person pay attention?

In the few local elections in the United States where Votes at 16 is in place, a uniquely American problem came to light. When looking at voting rates, differences were connected to how civics was taught in neighboring districts. In a district where civics was taught with voting clearly in mind, the voting rates of the 16–17-year-olds were very strong, but in a neighboring district they were dismal. The key difference was that in the second, civics was not taught as if the students would be voting soon, because the district was mixed with students from localities that did not have Votes at 16. This underlines the importance of civics, only if it is taught with a focus on elections and voting.[33] Where this was in place, the youngest cohorts outperformed their older cohorts by wide margins. To put this in perspective, local elections generally get the lowest turnouts in American politics.[34] This also points to the dangers of piecemeal reforms. They are likely to run into similar jurisdictional complications. But this should not get in the way of recognizing that this was an unscripted experiment to see how teaching civics with voting at the center can lead to improved voting rates.

IMPACT ON TEACHERS

Public school teachers are on the front line and will be directly impacted by this reform in civic education. Without them, this will not live up to its potential. If high school faculty are as resistant to fundamental change as are many college faculty, there will be predictable opposition, at least at the outset. On the other hand, most civics teachers understand that status quo civics is not effective.[35] They will have to adapt but they can look forward to more engaged students. The students will appreciate the relevance of material because it will prepare them for voting—a real world activity. One problem that confronts any proposed reform of civics education is that the percentage of civics, etc. classes taught by non-social science teacher education graduates is high. From a CIRCLE report, only 10 states require teachers of government or civics to be certified in civics or government.[36]

When Estonia decided to adopt Votes at 16, their alertness to the dangers of being partisan in their delivery of material allowed them to evade the "indoctrination" charges that will likely appear in the US debates.[37] The concern is that high school teachers, responsible for preparing their students to vote, will lead them toward their own preferred party—which is more than likely going to be Democratic.

In some of the more sobering passages in CIRCLE's report on state standards for civics requirements, they conclude,

> Our findings indicated that state standards give little support to teachers trying to navigate the ethical terrain that comes with teaching political ideologies. Indeed, the fact that no state standard clearly requires or encourages teachers to help students connect their own political views with the values and stances of the major parties supports that this is a controversial and difficult pedagogical issue for teachers.[38]

Some teachers might consider weaving current events into these courses in an effort to inject some relevance and excitement into the otherwise dry subject matter.[39] But many also fear that raising current political events in class runs too large a risk of provoking angry parental responses for trying to brainwash their child. As CIRCLE reported, "About one in four high school civics or American government teachers believe that the parents of their students or other adults in their community would object if they brought discussion of politics into the classroom."[40]

At one level, the charge is nearly impossible to deny—the whole purpose of education is to change what people know and the way people think. Evidence from colleges indicates that becoming more educated, while simultaneously maturing emotionally and intellectually, does cause many students to modify their political beliefs. But that evidence also shows that the percentage of students moving to the Left is nearly identical to the percentage of students moving to the Right.[41] Another study of college students found that 48 percent viewed liberalism more favorably than they did before college, and 50 percent viewed conservatism more favorably than before college. The symmetry also goes to those whose views of liberalism turned more negatively (30%) and those whose views of conservatism became more negative (31%).[42]

Below is the outline for the portion of an active civics class that focuses on helping students get registered and actually vote.

Active Civics Course outline—Becoming a Voter

- Constitutional Principles
- Voting History—Expansions of the Electorate
- Election History—Close ones
- Federalism
- Mechanics of Elections and Voting
- Registration
- Political Ideologies
- Political Parties
- Specific Election Issues
- Voting—Really!
- Reflection on being a full citizen
- Discussion of election results

A major question that can only be satisfactorily answered by the stakeholders is: Would more harm than good be done to require the new curriculum? In our federal system, it is very likely that answers would vary depending on what the particular state is currently requiring to be in civics course. One bright point is that not all states would have to conform to what my proposal demands. Our federal systems of education and elections give great latitude to states—they can accept this proposal, with or without changes to their civics requirements.

Within the context of Votes at 16, the main function of this active civics course is to reduce the costs of voting. The teacher will guide the students through the registration process, and help students understand when and where, and in certain states, how they can vote. The students will still have to get to the polling booth at the right time (unless schools bring polling booths to school, like they do at many colleges), and we would hope, they have to learn about issues and candidates. Teachers would assist in this aspect as well, thereby building the resources of these students. By making this a central part of the class, there is reason to hope that distractions can be contained. If this unfolds successfully, the first and most important step in building a habit of voting will be fully established.

Let us consider a hypothetical high school graduate who voted at 16 in the context of an active civics course but is not intending to go to college at age 18. As such this is a veteran voter who has successfully negotiated at least one election. This would provide that citizen with confidence that voting is something well within reach. That confidence should be high as long as the youth continues to live at home. Registration will not be necessary. The polling booth is very likely located in the same spot, with generally the same hours/days when voting is permissible. Even some of the candidates and issues will seem familiar.

If the young citizen moves away, there will be a lower probability of voting.[43] The relocated graduate would have to find out where the polling booth is and determine how to get there on election day. In both cases, that person will be aware that there are deadlines for registering to vote, and time periods when elections are open. To a greater degree than similarly aged citizens who have not yet voted, this graduate should have some understanding of the issues of the day, as well as the roles played by the government. Most importantly, we expect that these details would have been learned in civics class, and the student would have enjoyed the class more than in the past because of the clear relevance of that information for the student preparing to vote at 16.

CONCLUSION

This chapter explored the political landscape to sketch out the paths that might lead to the adoption of Votes at 16. It was unable to define a specific path because this reform is at an early stage of the process. It is not clear whether the injustice being suffered by 16–17-year-olds will overcome the inertia of the electoral status quo. By emphasizing how society will benefit from the greater equality and representativeness of our elections, advocates might gain the support of enough intellectuals and social elites to carry the day. The first step would be to get the issue as part of the national discussion.

The fate of the Equal Rights Amendment stands as a warning that passage is not assured even when the virtues of the reform are widely known with passionate advocates. The failure of the ERA was characterized as the result of opponents successfully forecasting that its passage would totally transform society's traditional male-female relationships. Casting the future in apocalyptic terms created enough doubt to stop what seemed like a sure success in its tracks. While this proposal is unlikely to confront such vehement challenges as did the ERA, the lesson is worth keeping in mind, that if you propose to change society, rather than just help out a particular group, you are proposing to change the status quo for everybody. Sometimes more modest claims are safer.

Then we turned to the important component that should accompany the Votes at 16 reform. Civics is and should be an important element in any effort to renew our political system. The story of civics is one with many critics and at least as many reformers intent on improving it. At the same time, civics sits on the margins of public education—pushed aside by STEM requirements. Here we cannot make strong commitments either. The subject is too complex for someone (me) untutored in the intricacies of public education. So, the suggestions are preliminary but the central role of civics to this proposal is undeniable.

As part of that goal of increasing engaged citizenship, the importance of quality civics education cannot be over-estimated. Milner recognizes that dropping the voting age to 16 in the context of a strong civics education system would benefit the young people who would otherwise be likely to drop out of the political system entirely. He is however unconvinced that the civics education in place is up to the task.[44]

Civic education seems caught between two basic options. One is to study the works of dead white men (founders) and the other is to take the students to where the masses are huddled at the local food kitchen. There is another option and that is to focus the education on the students themselves. Holbein and Hillygus have reached similar conclusions, though they focus exclusively on non-cognitive skills.[45] The proposal sketched out in these pages maintains that by connecting the mechanics of voting with the history of the expansion of voting rights, students will become more interested with and engaged in the traditional content of civics course. They are about to become adults and play adult roles and this will be symbolically and truly manifested in their preparation for the act of casting a real vote. In addition to having politically engaged voters we could also set our sights on having citizens who have a feeling of internal political efficacy, meaning they feel like they are indeed competent voters.

The analysis presented here operates on an assumption that the 16–17-year-old suffrage will come, perhaps state by state or by a congressionally initiated constitutional amendment. When that lower voting age is connected to high school civics classes, a habit of voting can be planted among a wider section of the American population, and it will address the very concerning decline in voting among White Americans with no college education. It is among that group in which the declines in voting rates are most severe.

Political parties will wonder whether they will benefit by bringing even younger voters into the voting booths. An important element to consider is that young people change their party registration but older voters rarely do.[46] Researchers have found that early life events have lasting impacts on the party identification of citizens decades later. For example, citizens whose formative years were shaped by the Great Depression tended to register as Democrats and continue that way. Similarly, citizens whose formative years were in the Eisenhower years, tended to register and continue as Republicans.[47] Not very long ago, it was standard that college-educated voters were strongly Republican. Non-college-educated voters were strongly Democratic. Both tendencies were rooted in economic factors. College education was the route to higher incomes and the GOP has traditionally favored cutting taxes on income. Meanwhile, labor unions were courted by and left to the tender mercies of the Democratic Party. As early as the 1980s pundits were discussing the rise of Reagan Democrats. These were working-class voters who had traditionally sided with the Democrats but switched to the Republicans. It is not that the parties have changed in any fundamental way, it is that the population has changed. Now college-educated voters are moving toward the Democrats, and the working-class voters are moving further into the Republican tent. The lesson is that these alignments are temporary which means it pays for parties to stay abreast of the changes.

Colleges are doing great things in increasing the voting rates of their students (although the resulting voting rates are still lackluster and trail their elders by wide margins), but this does not address the problem with non-college students. Dropping the voting age represents a step in that direction. In comparison to other reforms that are sensible and can have positive impacts on voting rates, this reform promises to have great impact because it addresses the problem at the root—young citizens who do not attend college are not developing the habit of voting. Instead they are developing the habit of not-voting.

Operating against this scenario is the long time required to have its impact work its way through the electorate. Generations will have to pass before the impact is full realized. Few political party leaders can afford to embrace near-term setbacks in exchange for success in 2050. The time-frame involved makes the danger seem overblown and also diminishes the appeal of the reform.

NOTES

1. Mycock, Andrew, Thomas Loughran, and Jonathan Tonge. "Understanding the Policy Drivers and Effects of Voting Age Reform." In *Lowering the Voting Age*

to 16: Learning from Real Experiences Worldwide, 43–63. Palgrave Studies in Young People and Politics. Palgrave Macmillan, 2020.

2. Brechenmacher. "Comparing Democratic Distress."

3. Lichtman. *The Embattled Vote in America*, 75.

4. Lichtman. *The Embattled Vote in America*, ch. 6, 147–79.

5. Lopez, German. "How the Voting Rights Act Transformed Black Voting Rights in the South, in One Chart." *Political Analysis. Vox.* Accessed March 13, 2020. https://www.vox.com/2015/3/6/8163229/voting-rights-act-1965

6. Manfedi, Christopher P. "Institutional Design and the Politics of Constitutional Modification: Understanding Failure in the United States and Canada." *Law & Society Review* 31, no. 1 (1997): 111–36. https://www.jstor.org/stable/3054096?seq =1#metadata_info_tab_contents

7. Cultice. *Youth's Battle for the Ballot.*

8. "Mission & Story." Political. March for our Lives, n.d. https://marchforourl ives.com/mission-story/

9. Roberts, Sam. "The Port Huron Statement at 50." *New York Times*, March 3, 2012, sec. New Analysis. https://www.nytimes.com/2012/03/04/sunday-review/the -port-huron-statement-at-50.html

10. Bauerlein, Mark. *The Dumbest Generation: How the Digital Age Stupefies Young Americans and Jeopardizes Our Future -- Or, Don't Trust Anyone under 30.* New York, NY: Penguin Group, 2008.

11. Franklin. *Voter Turnout and the Dynamics of Electoral Competition*; Milner. *The Internet Generation*; Hart and Youniss. *Renewing Democracy in Young America*; and "Public Support 'the Right to Vote at 16' More than 'Reducing the Voting Age from 18 to 16.'" Polling Organization. YouGov, n.d. https://yougov.co.uk/topi cs/politics/articles-reports/2018/05/23/public-support-right-vote-16-more-reducing -voting-

12. Marshall, John. "The Anti-Democrat Diploma: How High School Education Decreases Support for the Democratic Party." *American Journal of Political Science* 63, no. 1 (January 2019): 67–83. https://onlinelibrary.wiley.com/doi/full/10.1111/a jps.12409

13. "Reelection Rates Over the Years." Politicians & Elections. OpenSecrets.org: Center for Responsive Politics. Accessed February 14, 2020. https://www.opensecr ets.org/overview/reelect.php.

14. "Status and Trends in the Education of Racial and Ethnic Groups." Data. Institute of Education Sciences: National Center for Education Statistics, February 2019. https://nces.ed.gov/programs/raceindicators/indicator_RAA.asp

15. Fraga. *The Turnout Gap*, ch. 8, 195–212.

16. Schaffer, Frederic Charles. *The Hidden Costs of Clean Election Reform*, 159–87. Ithaca, NY: Cornell University, 2008.

17. Rafa, Alyssa, Dave Rogowski, Hunter Railey, Paul Baumann, and Stephanie Aragon. "50-State Comparison: Civic Education Policies." Research & Reports. Education Commission of the States, December 12, 2016. https://www.ecs.org/citiz enship-education-policies/

18. Achen and Bartels. *Democracy for Realists*, ch. 2, 21–51.

19. Hart and Youniss. *Renewing Democracy in Young America*, 64.

20. Jamieson, Kathleen Hall. "The Challenges Facing Civic Education in the 21st Century." *Daedalus* 142, no. 2 (2013): 65–83.

21. Hart and Youniss. *Renewing Democracy in Young America*, ch. 4, 59–86.

22. Rafac, Rogowski, Railey, Baumann, and Aragon. "50-State Comparison: Civic Education Policies."

23. Rafac, Rogowski, Railey, Baumann, and Aragon. "50-State Comparison: Civic Education Policies."

24. American Council of Trustees and Alumni. "A Crisis in Civic Education." ACTA, January 2016.

25. Hart and Youniss. *Renewing Democracy in Young America*, 61–9.

26. Pasek, Josh, Lauren Feldman, Daniel Romer, and Kathleen Hall Jamieson. "Schools as Incubators of Democratic Participation: Building Long-Term Political Efficacy with Civic Education." *Applied Developmental Science* 12, no. 1 (2008): 26–37. https://www.tandfonline.com/doi/abs/10.1080/10888690801910526

27. Commission on Youth Voting and Civic Knowledge. *All Together Now.*

28. Holbein and Hillygus. *Making Young Voters*, 128.

29. Shapiro, Sarah, and Catherine Brown. "The State of Civics Education." Education, K-12. Center for American Progress, February 21, 2018. https://www.americanprogress.org/issues/education-k-12/reports/2018/02/21/446857/state-civics-education/

30. Flaherty, Colleen. "And Civics Literacy For All." *Inside Higher Ed*, 24 2020, sec. News. https://www.insidehighered.com/news/2020/02/24/purdue-looks-adopt-civics-knowledge-undergraduate-requirement?utm_source=Inside+Higher+Ed&utm_campaign=d4d1bf6aa7-DNU_2019_COPY_02&utm_medium=email&utm_term=0_1fcbc04421-d4d1bf6aa7-197659373&mc_cid=d4d1bf6aa7&mc_eid=d69009e2ae

31. McAvoy, Paula, Rebecca Fine, and Ann Herrera. *State Standards Scratch the Surface of Learning about Political Parties and Ideology.* K-12 Schools and Civic Education, Center for Information & Research on Civic Learning & Engagement, Tufts University, 2016. https://circle.tufts.edu/sites/default/files/2020-01/WP81_StateStandardsPoliticalIdeoloy_2016.pdf

32. McAvoy, Fine, and Herrera. *State Standards Scratch*, 7.

33. Douglas. "Lowering the Voting Age from the Ground Up."

34. Douglas, "Lowering the Voting Age from the Ground Up."

35. Farkas, Steve, and Ann M. Duffett. "High Schools, Civics, and Citizenship: What Social Studies Teachers Think and Do." American Citizenship. American Enterprise Institute, September 2010. https://www.aei.org/research-products/working-paper/high-schools-civics-and-citizenship/

36. Commission on Youth Voting and Civic Knowledge. *All Together Now*, 11.

37. Toots and Idnurm. "Modernizing Voting in a Post-Transition Country," 167–87.

38. McAvoy, Fine, and Herrera. *State Standards Scratch*, 8.

39. Hart and Youniss. *Renewing Democracy in Young America*, ch. 4, 59–86.

40. Commission on Youth Voting and Civic Knowledge. *All Together Now*, 11.

41. Colby, Anne, Thomas Ehrlich, and Josh Corngold. *Educating for Democracy: Preparing Undergraduates for Responsible Political Engagement*, 11. Stanford, CA: The Carnegie Foundation for the Advancement of Teaching, 2010.

42. Mayhew, Matthew J., and Alyssa N. Rockenbach. "Does College Turn People into Liberals?" *The Conversation*, February 2, 2016. https://theconversation.com/do es-college-turn-people-into-liberals-90905

43. Highton, Benjamin. "Residential Mobility, Community Mobility, and Electoral Participation." *Political Behaviro* 22, no. 2, n.d.: 109–20. Accessed February 28, 2020. https://link.springer.com/article/10.1023%2FA%3A1006651130422

44. Milner. "Political Knowledge, Civic Education and Voting at 16," 65–79.

45. Holbein and Hillygus. *Making Young Voters.*

46. Hobbs, William R. "Major Life Events and the Age-Partisan Stability Association." *Political Behavior* 41 (June 7, 2018): 791–814. https://link.springer .com/content/pdf/10.1007/s11109-018-9472-6.pdf

47. Kaplan, Ethan, and Sharun Mukand. "The Persistence of Political Partisanship: Evidence from 9/11," November 15, 2010. https://warwick.ac.uk/fac/soc/economics/ staff/swmukand/ideologypersistence11-15.pdf

Chapter 6

Wrapping Up

It is time to see what we have discovered on this journey that began long ago with a simple discussion question in an Introduction to Political Science course. Along the way, we discovered that:

- There are no compelling reasons to deny the vote to 16–17-year-olds. Reasons for denying it to them could as easily be applied to deny the vote to others. The clearest example is the claim that young ones do not know enough about politics. Most Americans score very low on all sorts of political knowledge scales, and yet they are allowed to vote.
- There is convincing evidence that in terms of voting rates, 16–17-year-olds outperform 18–21-year-olds. This empirical evidence supports our theoretical thoughts about whether 16–17-year-olds are capable of voting in a responsible fashion.
- Dropping the voting age to 18 in 1971 might have been a mistake in terms of voting rates. This does not mean, however, that it was a mistake in all senses of the matter. Young people who did begin voting earlier under the Votes at 18 Amendment gained psychologically and in terms of political efficacy.
- The reason that Votes at 18 might have been a mistake is due to the habitual nature of voting and non-voting. There are intuitive and empirical reasons to believe this may be the case. Most obvious is that 18 seems to be an inappropriate time to try to instill a positive habit since many people at that age are in the midst of personal transitions that are generally considered of greater importance than casting a vote in a primary or general election.
- Among the ways we consider the motivation to vote are the "costs" of voting. These include the registration process which is more demanding than the actual voting. Finding and getting to the polling both on a workday are

117

other types of costs that American voters generally must pay, though some states are allowing ballots to be submitted by mail. For young voters, the costs are highest when the habit of voting is lowest or nonexistent. As citizens become veteran voters the costs of voting decrease.

- The United States is not unique but it is extreme in the extent to which education levels are connected to voting rates. In effect, one of the underappreciated bonuses to getting a college education is that the person is very likely to become a lifetime voter. This is the pattern around the democratic world (excluding the compulsory voting countries), but what is, in this author's opinion, the most important point is that there is a penalty associated with not getting a college degree. That person is likely to never become a regular voter. And, we discovered that over the last few decades this penalty has become more pronounced. We also learned that this penalty is most evident among White Americans and less evident in other racial categories.
- Civics classes are of low priority and of limited effectiveness in producing increased political knowledge and political participation (especially in voting). We recognized that civics classes have several important features that make them integral to Votes at 16. First, they are taken by nearly all young Americans, regardless of whether they are planning to attend college or select another path. This enhances the potential for civics to become a vital source of sparking political interest and voting. By seeking to capitalize on this potential by injecting into these courses steps that help young citizens pay the "costs" of registering and voting for the first time, we anticipate that students will respond positively to the enhanced relevance of the civics courses and embrace the opportunity to shed their status as proto-citizens and exercise their rights to cast real votes for real candidates in real elections.
- As this process unfolds, we can expect two positive outcomes. One is that voting rates will climb, albeit very slowly. The youngest voters will not be pulling down the overall voting rates any longer. If habits of voting are established early and maintained (as habits generally are), then young voters will raise the overall voting rates. The second is that the voting electorate will more closely correspond to the composition of the public. Instead of the upper-class accent, perhaps the heavenly chorus will begin to incorporate some syncopated beats, with decidedly salsa flavors.
- Votes at 16 can solve the voting puzzle—that our wealthy, aging, and increasingly educated population should be raising the voting rates, yet the voting rates are falling. By spreading the voting habit as equally across the entire population as we can, Votes at 16 and its associated active civics can help reverse this trend.
- The addition of new and more diverse young voters will invigorate elections and cause politicians and political parties to shift some of their attention

toward this new group of voters. Politicians respond to high-voting groups, and if Votes at 16 is implemented we can expect that young voters will vote at higher levels than in the past, thereby earning greater attention from political parties. In turn this will encourage a shift of public policy in the directions preferred by younger voters.

- The path to adoption of this reform can take two paths or a combination of both. States can lead the way by adopting Votes at 16 themselves. As this process unfolds there might be a snowballing effect. As one state, preferably a big and influential one, adopts this reform, pressure will build on other states to follow suit. As more states adopt the reform, the pressure on the others continues to build. As the process continues, pressure will begin to build on Capitol Hill. Representatives from states that have adopted the reform will likely lead the charge in building momentum toward a constitutional amendment. Alternatively, the process may begin at the national level. As the national debate unfolds, advocates in states will use those debates to show skeptics that the reform is not crazy.

- An invigorated American political system can serve as a positive model for democratic activists around the world. When our system is in disarray and seems to be tottering, the belief in others around the world in the superiority of liberal democracy is weakened. Votes at 16 in the United States can help reverse this.

THE REST OF THE STORY

Just as there are several points in favor of this proposed reform, there are critical questions that are raised as well. Here we will raise these questions and provide responses.

- *Chances are zero, thus not worth the effort. The Republican Party will refuse to approve this reform and in general the tide is running against expanding the voting rolls and even democracy itself is under siege.* There is truth in the general description. However, the conclusion to be drawn from it is in doubt. Two responses can be made to the claim that if something is not going to get approved it is worthless to pursue it. One is that, sometimes, unlikely things happen. About two years before the Berlin Wall fell, a German political scientist told me that nothing remotely like that was going to happen for a long, long time. Larsen et al. discovered that when Votes at 16 is run as an experiment, there can be up to 5 percent increase in the citizens' support for national legislation to drop the voting age. It seems that evidence that 16–17-year-olds can vote responsibly allows skeptical voters to gain comfort with the idea.[1] The other response is to say that when the tide is against expanding democracy, that is precisely the right time to engage in that fight. Sometimes resisting something that is negative requires more than battling the negative; it requires creating a positive vision as an alternative.

- *A related problem, from the perspective of critics, is that the impact will be limited.* There will still be a voting gap between students who graduate and go to college and those who do not go to college. Any improvement will be marginal and will be very unlikely to change any policy outcomes. The response to this is that this is certainly a possibility. But we will not know until it is tried and tested for a generation or more. Most of our evidence is recent and we do not have much long-term evidence from the South American countries that have had Votes at 16 the longest. So, it is too early to tell. Because the young and the poor are most sensitive to changes in rules, the prospects for this reform changing voting behaviors are optimistic. This is because change is more possible among young people. A 50-year-old non-voter is unlikely to begin voting no matter how easy it becomes to vote. This is because that non-voter is a habitual non-voter, and habits, good or bad, can be tough to break. The difference with the youth is that non-voting is not a habit. But, hanging out with non-voting young friends is a recipe for a lifetime of non-voting that too many young people currently follow. However, when there are reforms directed especially at the youth, they can be responsive: "this suggests that young people are more sensitive to factors affecting turnout across countries."[2]

It is a reasonable question of how simply adding a limited and likely low-voting segment of the population to the voting rolls is going to generate many positive changes. In addition to the specific arguments that have already been made here, it is worth reading the words of one of the charismatic, inspirational, assassinated leaders of our past. In 1966 Senator Robert Kennedy gave a speech in Cape Town, South Africa, in which he spoke of the power of small beginnings to effect great change:

> It is from numberless diverse acts of courage such as these that the belief that human history is thus shaped. Each time a man stands up for an ideal, or acts to improve the lot of others, or strikes out against injustice, he sends forth a tiny ripple of hope, and crossing each other from a million different centers of energy and daring those ripples build a current which can sweep down the mightiest walls of oppression and resistance.[3]

In more prosaic terminology this means that even if we do not see the results immediately, doing the right thing will pay off in the long run.

- *People of that age are not prepared to fulfill the role of citizen.* This does not seem to be the case based on evidence drawn from locations where Votes at 16 has been in place. Although the evidence is still rather skimpy, the evidence is almost consistently pointing in the direction opposed to this criticism. Wagner et al. reported in their survey of Austrian 16–17-year-olds a surprising finding that young people have significantly higher trust in institutions than older voters. This result holds not only when compared to the 18–21 age group but they also outperform the 22–25 and 26–30 and 31+ age groups.[4]

- *Civic education cannot bear the weight of what the reform proposes to place on it, and furthermore, jamming the existing civics courses with these elements necessarily means that other, more worthwhile, elements must be replaced, thereby lessening the overall value of the courses.* This is a legitimate concern, and the tide we mentioned earlier certainly seems to be running strongly against proposals to expand the place of civics in public education. A local education official told me that society seems to look to schools to fix all the ills facing society. He quickly acknowledged that he did not think that was a problem related to civics. Against this we have the expectation that faculty and students will respond favorably to the inclusion of hands-on political information. Once established, the active civics courses should be fun for teachers and students alike.

- *If implemented, it will contribute to the existing bias in the education-voting arena.* The claim here is that as in so many other things, the students from the most advanced schools will receive the best mentoring and inspiration. This will increase their likelihood to become regular voters. Meanwhile the less fortunate students will not see much increase in their likelihood of voting. Consequently, the gap between the two groups, which is already substantial and growing, will get an extra boost from this reform. In response, we acknowledge that the gaps referred to exist and have been devilishly difficult to eliminate despite countless efforts by educators. Where we part ways is on the question of whether the benefits of this reform would automatically flow toward the most fortunate. The criticism suggests a belief that nothing will help bridge the gap, or push up low voting rates among youth. The reform promises higher turnout by reducing costs and building resources, even if only marginally among poor youth, and is thus worth the risk. A number of studies have shown that low-income and non-White students benefit more from certain imaginative efforts to promote political engagement. Partly this is because the fortunate youth will be inclined to become regular voters, so the reform will not move their numbers up very much. In contrast, youth from the less advantaged groups have lots of room to grow. Thus, we can expect the gap to close, not to widen.

- *A variant of this claims that greater civic education efforts in high school would increase the participation bias because it will only work on those students already interested in politics.*[5] This is plausible only if the civics courses are designed simply to heighten student interest in politics. If the civics courses are structured to prepare these citizens to vote, the preexisting variation in political interest should dissipate if not disappear completely (which is a good thing).

- *Even if it works, it will tackle one problem but allow a more troubling problem to persist: Voters are not knowledgeable or interested enough.* Even though there are some bold claims of the positive effect from this reform, there is no claim to solve all problems. But there is a claim that the revised version of civics which will connect directly to the process of registering and voting will excite students and generate more than normal interest in the platforms of the political parties, the institutions of government, and other related matters. If we begin to inculcate these positive experiences into successive generations of Americans, we can anticipate that it will generate a more positive orientation toward the political system. Recall that young people tend to harbor more optimism than older voters under the current status quo. Yet some of them despair of getting involved in politics and government, because they do not understand how they work. A re-energized civics curriculum could deliver the knowledge that young people need.

- *There are other, more easily achievable reforms that would at least get something accomplished. It would be better to focus on them first.* These other proposals are sensible and worth pursuing in the near term. However, the Votes at 16 proposal is superior to these in that it promises to expand the electorate into populations that have traditionally voted at low levels. This is because only Votes at 16 is premised on rooting the first voting experience in high school civics classes. Thus, it alone promises to put the habit of voting into the behaviors of citizens who encompass the near-universal range of citizens: poor and rich; non-college and college bound; non-White and White.

- *I know my little brother should not be allowed to vote!* This is perhaps the most common objection, though we could substitute sister/son/daughter for brother in the sentence depending on the family. As we have noted several times, there is evidence to suggest 16–17-year-olds are smart enough, knowledgeable enough, and mature enough to vote responsibly. It does not necessarily mean that your little brother/sister/son/daughter is smarter or more knowledgeable or more mature than you are. They just have to be smart and knowledgeable and mature enough to vote. But, yes, your (fill in the blank) is not smart enough to vote.

PROJECTIONS OF PAST AND FUTURE ELECTIONS

It is unwise and perhaps impossible to conceive of a dramatic political reform such as this one, without contemplating how it would impact elections moving forward. The problem, as with all large-scale social scientific predictions, is that there are so many variables that can impact future elections; it is necessary to issue a caveat beforehand that states something akin to "as long as nothing else changes . . . here is what will change." As inadequate as this formulation is, without a time machine or without great advances in artificial intelligence, we are limited in what we can claim with confidence.

So, for this project we must identify the elements that will change and focus almost entirely on them, even though we know full well that future election results will hinge on matters far beyond our reach here, such as the health of the economy and the rise of new or different political alliances and leaders. Here our target is the change that adding 16–17-year-olds to the voting rolls will have on presidential election outcomes.

We will concentrate on the presidential election for two primary reasons. One, it is the election that most citizens know the most about. Two, is that the results will be more dramatic than calculating House or Senate races. Presidential races can be decided by a single state switching its Electoral College Votes from one party to the other.

This requires clear statements of our assumptions about the size and political distribution of this cohort. At the outset, it is important to note that the 2016 presidential election was stark in the different voting preferences of the age groups, as shown in Table 6.1. Large voting margins in favor of Donald Trump among the oldest cohorts carried the day. Young voters were decidedly cool to the Republican presidential candidate. Also, note that the younger voters were much more apt to opt for third-party candidates than were older voters.

Table 6.1 Presidential Vote by Age from the 2016 Exit Polls

Age	Clinton (%)	Trump (%)	Other (%)
18–29	55	36	9
30–44	51	41	8
34–64	44	52	4
65+	45	52	3

Source: Made by author from CNN exit polls.
NOTE: We assume that all future young cohorts have the same ideological/partisan leanings as the 18–24-year-olds did in 2016. We also assume that all future cohorts will turnout at the 2016 levels.[14]

Obligatory Caveats: Why this projection will not be accurate.[6]

1) The bane of the existence of social scientists is that unlike falling rocks or rushing rivers, people modify their behaviors in response to changing conditions. Politically this means that when the partisan pendulum shifts too far in one direction, it has an inherent tendency to come back toward a temporary equilibrium. This is expressed differently in different realms. Parties and their base constituencies will vary over time. They will naturally modify their appeals to garner as much of the youth vote as possible.

2) Youth are not always going to be much more liberal than older voters. Think of the youth coming of age during the Reagan years. Partisanship of people changes as they age—very slowly, of course.

3) As generational experts point out, formative events shape generations. Things like major wars, economic collapses, and natural disasters have pushed new cohorts of voters into patterns that they maintain throughout their voting careers. Some of these events will surely happen prior to 2048. One is happening as this is being written. COVID-19 could be the type of event that shapes the partisan orientation of an entire generation.

EVALUATING THE 2016 ELECTION AND BEYOND

It is not by itself surprising that the first future election in 2020 is projected to have three states flip to the Democrats. The 2016 election was very close and the outcome famously rode on the back of 80,000 votes between the three

Table 6.2 Projecting the Future with 16–17-Year-Old's Voting

Year	Newly Flipped	Total Flipped	Electoral College	Similarity
2016 Real			D-232 – R-306	JFK 1960 (303–219)
2016	Michigan 16	16	D-248 – R-290	GWB 2004 (286–251)
2020 Wave 1	Wisconsin 10 Pennsylvania 20	46	D-278 – R-260	WW 1916 (277–254)
2024	Florida 29	75	D-307 – R-231	DT 2016 (306–232)
2028	No Change	75	D-307 – R-231	DT 2016 (306–232)
2032	No Change	75	D-307 – R-231	DT 2016 (306–232)
2036 Wave 2	Arizona 11 North Carolina 15	101	D-333 – R-205	BO 2012 (332–206)
2040	Georgia 16	117	D-349 – R-189	BO 2008 (365–173)
2044 Wave 3	Ohio 18 Texas 38	173	D-405 – R-133	GHWB 1988 (426–111)
2048	Iowa 6	179	D-411 – R-127	GHWB 1988 (426–111)

Source: Projections done by the author from CNN exit polls

states (Michigan, Pennsylvania, and Wisconsin) that are projected to switch to Democratic in 2020. Though not entirely surprising, it is still instructive to recognize that this project has the Democrats winning in 2020s presidential race.

An important feature of this projection is time. By 2024, the 2016 Electoral College vote gap will be reversed. But it will take until 2036 before the electoral map is definitively pro-Democratic. In 2036, North Carolina will become the first Southern state (other than Florida) to flip to the Democrats. The year 2036 also represents what I would call the Second Wave. The year 2044 represents what I call the Third Wave. The biggest election change will happen in 2044 with 56 electoral votes going toward the Democrats.

The table extends through 8 elections covering 32 years. During that time, only 10 states flip from Democratic to Republican. Meanwhile 19 states remain in the Republican column despite the addition of several cohorts of Left-leaning younger voters. Among the states that would NOT turn to the Democrats but stay loyally Republican are Alabama, Alaska, Arkansas, Idaho, Kansas, Kentucky, Louisiana, Mississippi, Missouri, Montana, Nebraska, North Dakota, Oklahoma, South Carolina, South Dakota, Tennessee, Utah, West Virginia, and Wyoming. Those 19 states total a mere 126 electoral votes that only account for roughly 24 percent of electoral votes.

The outcomes will next be evaluated from the perspective of those who endorse the reform as well as those who are skeptical of the proposal. Advocates might rejoice at the quick flip of the Electoral College in the very first future race. The reform clearly has an impact. Meanwhile, slow and limited change places advocates in a predicament. On the one hand, advocates would be impatient with the lack of a sudden transformation, and on the other hand, they might appreciate the slow accretion of changes that are not so extreme as to provoke a backlash, and whose cumulative effects might be substantial.

Opponents will be firmer in their opposition. They will shudder at the idea of turning over important decisions to the least knowledgeable voters who are also the most volatile in their partisan loyalties. And if the impacts would come quickly that would not give the democratic institutions much time to adapt, making the changes abrupt. They would maintain that anyone in the middle who is entertaining the proposal as a potentially innocuous change, should take a second or third look.

Gallego notes that voting turnout rates are very slow to change, as the old folks continue voting/not voting regardless of changes in the system, whereas young people can be influenced more by those changes.[7] The time is slowed with this particular reform because the high-voting 65+ age group will be exiting the scene, to be replaced by lower-voting 65+ voters. So, whereas Fraga examined the evidence on race, in which the Whitest generations are gradually being replaced by less-White generations, in the case of age, the departing groups are the highest voting groups.[8]

PROJECTIONS—TWINS

After looking at projections based on numbers, we will now turn to a projection of sorts that will look at the qualitative aspects of the reform and its associated active civics component. As a means of depicting the impact of this reform, dropping the voting age to 16 and revising civics courses to support this, we will utilize a hypothetical scenario of twins who vary by their educational plans and by whether or not they were part of Votes at 16. The impact of factors such as costs, resources, distractions, and habits can perhaps be seen more vividly through the employment of fictitious twins who differ on only one important criteria at a time. We will conduct the following twin comparisons.

A) Current 18 College vs. Current 18 Non-College. This will illustrate the status quo, and how it is skewed in favor of the College student.
B) Reform 16 College vs. Reform 16 Non-College. This will illustrate the impact of dropping the voting age to 16, for college and non-college students.
C) Reform 16-Non-College vs. Current 18 Non-College. This will illustrate the impact of the reform on the non-college student population. This will reveal how the most at-risk demographic group will be affected.

TWINS SCENARIO A—STATUS QUO

Imagine identical twins separated at birth (or just any two normal people of the same age).[9] One we will call Chuck, who was born into a two-parent family with both parents having college degrees and are regular voters. There are books in the house, the family watches news programs, etc. Chuck plans for and attends college where he majors in a social science or humanity discipline. When he turns 18, he is immediately approached about registering to vote. He does, and when election times come, he votes.

The second twin we will call Jack, who grew up in a working-class household. Neither parents went to college and one has been a registered voter but cannot remember casting a vote. The family does not watch much news, and there are few books for adults anywhere. Jack heads to the local truck company to pursue his ambitions of being a truck driver. When Jack turns 18 no one notices that he is now eligible to register and vote, and Jack does neither.

Because Jack is curious about the world around him, he does follow the news episodically. Because he will gradually learn more about the political system and the issues of the day, and because he will likely get married and have kids with all of their attendant issues, he has a fair chance of becoming a voter later in life. Eventually, taxes, school funding, and college costs will begin to show him that government policies and decisions have direct bearing on his family's opportunities.

TWINS SCENARIO B—REFORM COLLEGE AND REFORM NON-COLLEGE

Now, let us imagine that these twins were attending high school when the voting age is dropped to 16, meaning they would be in the first wave of new voters. They are both enrolled in a civics class that is required to graduate from high school. What impact would this have on the two young twins? Both will have their voting costs reduced substantially by the civics course instructor. The instructor will lay out the vagaries of voting registration and provide them with information necessary for clearing this hurdle. The instructor will inform all of the students about the date of the upcoming election, and where the students would be able to vote. They will also learn about what the process of voting entails: is it mail-in, is there early voting, what type of identification is necessary, etc. Ultimately, the civics class would cover some of the topics that seem central to the upcoming election.

Chuck will accept all of this assistance and will do research on his own on the candidates who interest him most. He will successfully vote in his first election while in high school. However, the fact that college is typically a brand-new location, acts to depress his likelihood of voting. When he gets to college, he will have to decide on whether to keep his home registration or re-register at his college location. His college will provide him with proper (we hope) legal advice on this, which like much else involving elections, varies from state to state. The fact that Chuck is still in school raises his likelihood of voting. By the time Chuck graduates college, he is well on his way to having a solid habit of voting and when he moves to his new job, he will relatively quickly and successfully change his registration to his new location. One or two more elections will effectively insure that Chuck will become a lifetime voter.

Jack will also accept the assistance and perform his civic duty while in high school. But what happens when he graduates high school? Will his experience cause him to continue voting and take whatever necessary steps necessary to keep his registration legal? Or will he succumb to the stereotypical young voter who is unlikely to vote? There are some positive and some negative aspects to answering this question.

On the negative side, he is likely to be hanging out with young people who are not likely to be committed to voting. Politics is something they might not discuss except when they make a youthful cynical comment about the corruption of a politician or the entire political system. Jack may be dating someone he is thinking about marrying. This can occupy 90 percent of the mind of many people. Is marriage the right thing now? Where would we live? How will we pay rent and all the other expenses? Perhaps, Jack is lucky and this works out and produces a beautiful new citizen. Now the pressure is on and the questions multiply, including where to live because the choice of school district is so important. But enough of that. This discussion is meant to suggest that Jack may have a lot on his mind except politics and will likely not be surrounded by people discussing politics and elections all the time. This suggests that Jack will not become a life-long voter, at least at this stage of his life.

But there are several positive things that need to be considered. One is that the costs for voting the second time are going to be lower than the first time, especially if Jack still lives at home. In fact, Chuck who has left home to attend college is at a disadvantage here. But having voted once, Jack should be confident that on his own he can once again navigate the voting process. Another positive aspect will be that his civics class might have sparked an interest in politics that had been latent to that point. Jack was not inclined to study history because it was as someone said "just one damn thing after another," but because the civics was tied to his voting he understood the importance of the historical origins and roots of our democracy. He found it much more interesting to discuss matters that were related to the votes he would cast that very semester.

Another possible positive influence on this is that Jack's excitement about becoming a registered voter and then wearing with sheepish pride his "I Voted" sticker after casting his first ballot, might translate into new interest in politics by his parents.[10] Thus, Jack's voting rights could trickle-up to the generation above him. And, if so, they could all support each other in continuing to vote moving forward.

Finally, Jack as a registered voter and one who has voted, belongs to a cohort that would be of greater interest to political parties. Political parties these days are not much interested in young people since they vote at very low rates. It is almost always more economical to target older citizens with their political campaigns. But Jack and Chuck represent a new youth generation who have already voted, and would seem ripe for switching to a new party in the new election. Political parties like old people because they tend to vote. One thing that parties don't like about old people (of the opposition party) is that they are set in their ways. Young people, on the other hand, are subject to dramatic changes in political philosophy. A young big-government liberal can become a libertarian for a while and then transition to a national security conservative about as quickly as college students change academic majors. It is this variability that makes them so appealing to political campaigns. Those in our camp need to be nourished sufficiently with promises and attention to keep them from straying, and those in the opposite camp are ripe for being seduced to our side. This is true only if these young voters can be expected to vote more frequently than their older cohorts.

TWINS SCENARIO C—REFORM NON-COLLEGE AND CURRENT NON-COLLEGE

This scenario differs from the first two because it isolates the impact of the reform on the population that is at highest risk for developing into habitual non-voters. As we have established, these youth tend to have limited political knowledge and face the costs of voting on their own. Because the non-reform non-college student has not been guided along the path of registration and voting, and whose exposure to politics is likely to have been distasteful, chances are low that he/she will vote in their first age-eligible election, and might not evolve into a habitual voter later in life. Contrast this with the reform of non-college citizens. It is possible that the exposure to civics/American politics might be relatively pleasant since it seems connected to what that student will soon be undertaking—moving into the role of a voting citizen. With a more pleasant view of politics, this citizen might develop a greater interest in learning more about the context and nature of our political system.

It is worth noting here that nothing magical is assumed. Young voters will still tend to see the political system as a dismal place of partisan bickering. In this way they would probably mimic their older fellow citizens. Where they might differ is that they might have more faith in the institutions of government to maintain general stability. And as *Running from Office* shows there is a correlation between learning about the principles and the institutions of the political system and retaining a desire to engage with that system to overcome the dysfunctional aspects that deter many of their less political knowledgeable cohorts.[11] In combination, these two characteristics represent the traditional strand of optimism and desire to improve the world that we associate with youth.

LESSONS FROM THE TWINS

The scenarios highlighted the impact of high costs coupled with low resources. They illustrated the changes that can flow from active civics. They showed that the reformed college students will vote even more than they currently do. In fact, we can expect that the gap across majors will be reduced. Moreover, one might argue that more politically engaged STEM majors would be good as they could be better prepared to bring scientific perspectives to political issues. More directly linked to the argument in this book, it shows that the reformed twins will vote at much closer rates than the status quo twins. We would expect that their voting rates should converge, if we assume that the increase in reformed college voting rates is less than the increase in reformed non-college voting rates.

An important point can be made at this point that the twins exercise was conducted with the racial identity of the protagonists being omitted. But we know that the racial composition of the average status quo college is different from the average non-college status quo. When we add these elements to the picture, we can see that the reform will narrow the gap between the races. Between the two projections we get a compelling view that this reform would have positive impacts. At the same time, both exercises have significant caveats. The election projection to 2048 assumes that lowering the costs and building the resources will generate greater turnout results. The twin scenarios assume that taking active civics will reduce the voting gap between college and non-college populations.

OUR JOURNEY

This book first recapitulated the series of discoveries that guided this expedition. Then it shifted gears to conduct an extended analysis of the proposed reform itself. It examined the steps that adoption might entail, drawing upon historical antecedents. It continued to estimate the impact of expanding the youth vote from the 2016 election to 2020 and beyond. This path parallels in some degree the transition between little-j justice and Big-J Justice.

We traveled from a simple question to an innocuous reform to a radical improvement in the political status quo, potentially. Along the way my thinking evolved. First it was focused on what I call the little-j justice dimensions. Early on it seemed to my student and me that there were not really any persuasive reasons behind the resistance to dropping the voting age. As we learned about American voting history, we realized that skeptics have always doubted whether the new group possesses the personal qualities that democracy demands. We understood that skepticism is natural and necessary. And, just as often we found that when the proposed group could vote they acquitted themselves quite well. Women and African Americans have essentially caught up with the voting rates of the White American males who had maintained a tight grip on voting. Later our hunch was revealed to be true in the case of countries where Votes at 16 has been instituted and therefore provides us with data to use to assess the quantity and quality of 16–17-year-old voting behaviors. Slowly, over several years, as this evidence began to trickle in, my thinking began to escalate toward what I call Big-J Justice. This involves anything that would benefit anyone beyond the 16–17-year-olds themselves. One of the earliest discoveries was learning that voting and non-voting are habits. From there it was easy to understand Mark Franklin's point that 18 is the wrong time to begin forming habits. For modern Americans 18 is typically a period of profound transition. When one's life is in transition it is probably more common to develop bad habits than good habits. This certainly seems to be the case for voting. Perhaps because I have been safely ensconced in academia, I may have been unaware of the lack of support given to the 18+ age group in terms of encouragement to vote. Especially as a Political Scientist I was mostly in the company of politically engaged young people. When I normally interact with young people outside the academy, we rarely get to the point of asking each other our voting patterns. But once this came to my attention, I could not easily let it go.

What began with a nearly whimsical look at a little-j justice issue, granting the right to vote to 16–17- year-olds became a Big-J Justice issue when considering the impact of this reform on the inequality of voting in the United States. This reform promises to expand the voting population while decreasing the gaps in voting and in the process increasing the overall turnout rates, albeit slowly. If active civics generates greater student excitement, we might even see improvements in our lackluster national scores on political knowledge.

Now, we see that the reform has even broader implications. In the eyes of many sober political analysts, American democracy is in some degree of peril, and this is part of a global trend. While the troubles facing the American political system will not be solved by expanding and equalizing the voting rolls, there is little doubt that if the results forecast here come true, that it will signal that democracy is on the mend. And this, in turn, will send a message around the globe that democracy is not fatally flawed and on its way to the ash heap of history.

The future sketched by the last chapter and this concluding chapter have, naturally, focused on the specific aspects of the proposal. Now, it is appropriate to step back for a broader perspective. This book is appearing at a time of dire projections for the American political system, and democracy elsewhere around the globe. These words are being penned during the opening stages of COVID-19 (March 21, 2020) in the United States. It is impossible from this vantage point to forecast its political impacts, but one suspects they will be profound. The shock of 9/11 in 2001 left an indelible mark on our politics, in both the foreign and domestic arenas. Domestically, we have ceded much authority to our government to monitor our behaviors in the name of identifying and stopping terrorists. Internationally, we reserve to ourselves the right to attack terrorists via drone strikes and to coerce or overthrow governments we suspect are harboring terrorists. Whatever comes from the COVID-19 will be different but might be equally profound.

This is all the more reason, in my opinion, that the time for Votes at 16 is fast approaching. American politics needs an infusion of optimism and creativity. We need it to dampen our own cynicism and pessimism. And it can be argued that the world needs the United States to strike a confident and optimistic pose. One bold way to do this is to embrace a high-profile reform in the name of Votes at 16. We would not be the first country to do so, but certainly we would be the most important.

It is not that the 16–17-year-olds are endowed with extraordinary wisdom, or even the ability to pass a citizenship test. No, they are just an ordinary cadre of kids with high ambitions and self-doubt. The task we are setting for them—to preserve and renew our democracy—is a tall order. This is precisely why we need contributions from all of them. There is a phrase that I came upon to the effect of "our society would be judged not by how it served children but by how it challenged its youth to serve society."[12] When these types of wise and inspirational statements are made, there is a tendency to think about the youth who are headed to Yale, Harvard, or the University of Chicago, all prepped and ready to make their marks on the world. In our quieter moments, perhaps we also think about the humbler students heading for one of the directional campuses that comprise much of our state university systems. Only rarely, when we think of the next generation's stars, do we think of the numerous youth who will never get a college degree. What do we expect from them? Aside from military and first-responder service, my guess is not much.

When scholars shine their lights on the innovative approaches to politics by young people, or as Milner calls them "netizens" they typically have in mind college-educated folks.[13] These are the kids I teach, and I care for them and I am concerned for their future. But what has sustained me on this long journey is the understanding that this reform has a genuine chance to reduce the political inequality which has steadily marginalized those who do not have college degrees. Sure, the companies and everything else will still be run by the graduates of Yale, Harvard, and Chicago. But the reform will allow the non-college folks to use their democratic levers at the ballot box to hold those elites accountable. Many of these folks will become more actively engaged in their communities as well. We need to harness all the constructive energies that entire young generations have in abundance.

NOTES

1. Larsen, Levinsen, and Kjaer. "Democracy for the Youth?"
2. Gallego. *Unequal Political Participation Worldwide*, 49.
3. Kennedy, Robert. "Day of Affirmation Address," June 6, 1966. https://www.jfklibrary.org/learn/about-jfk/the-kennedy-family/robert-f-kennedy/robert-f-kennedy-speeches/day-of-affirmation-address-university-of-capetown-capetown-south-africa-june-6-1966.
4. Wagner and Kritzinger. "Voting at 16."
5. Wattenberg. *Is Voting for Young People?*, 199.
6. CNN. "Exit Polls."
7. Gallego. *Unequal Political Participation Worldwide*, 48–9.
8. Fraga. *The Turnout Gap.*
9. Lahtinen, Hannu, Jani Erola, and Hanna Wass. "Sibling Similarities and the Importance of Parental Socioeconomic Position in Electoral Participation." *Social Forces* soz010 (May 2019). https://academic.oup.com/sf/article/98/2/702/5365291
10. Dahlgaard, Jens Olav. "Trickle Up Political Socialization: The Causal Effect on Turnout of Parenting a Newly Enfranchised Voter." *American Political Science Review* 112, no. 3: 698–705. Accessed July 10, 2018. https://search.proquest.com/docview/2063714620/fulltext/A166888BB14C4704PQ/16?accountid=14968
11. Lawless and Fox. *Running From Office*, 140–3.
12. Hart, Daniel, and Youniss. *Renewing Democracy in Young America*, 83, quote attributed to Katharine Lenroot.
13. Milner. *The Internet Generation*, 67–70.
14. CNN. "Exit Polls." *News*, November 23, 2016. https://www.cnn.com/election/2016/results/exit-polls

Bibliography

2018 Election Center. Education. CIRCLE. Accessed March 13, 2020. https://circle. tufts.edu/2018-election-center.

Achen, Christopher, and Larry Bartels. "Democracy for Realists: Holding up a Mirror to the Electorate." *Juncture* 22, no. 4 (2016): 269–75. https://doi.org/10.1111/j .2050-5876.2016.00873.x

———. *Democracy for Realists: Why Elections Do Not Produce Responsive Government*. Princeton, NJ: Princeton University Press, 2016.

Aichholzer, Julian, and Sylvia Kritzinger. "Voting at 16 in Practice; A Review of the Austrian Case." In *Lowering the Voting Age to 16: Learning from Real Experiences Worldwide*, edited by Jan Eichhorn and Johannes Berg, 81–101. Palgrave Studies in Young People and Politics. Palgrave Macmillan, 2020.

Alexander, Michelle. *The New Jim Crow: Mass Incarceration in the Age of Colorblindness*. New York, NY: The New Press, 2012.

Alter, Charlotte, Suyin Haynes, and Justin Worland. "Time 2019 Person of the Year — Greta Thunberg." *Time*, December 23, 2019. https://time.com/person-of-the-year -2019-greta-thunberg/

American Council of Trustees and Alumni. "A Crisis in Civic Education." ACTA, January 2016.

American Democracy Project. Educational. American Association of State Colleges and Universities. Accessed March 5, 2020. https://www.aascu.org/programs/ADP/

Amy, Douglas J. "Instant Runoff Voting." Political. FairVote, February 15, 2020. https://www.fairvote.org/instant_runoff_voting_no_substitute_for_pr

Anderson, Carol. *One Person, No Vote: How Voter Suppression Is Destroying Our Democracy*. New York, NY: Bloomsbury Publishing, 2018.

Bauerlein, Mark. *The Dumbest Generation: How the Digital Age Stupefies Young Americans and Jeopardizes Our Future — Or, Don't Trust Anyone under 30*. New York, NY: Penguin Group, 2008.

Beck, Paul Allen, and M. Kent Jennings. "Lowering the Voting Age: The Case of the Reluctant Electorate." *Public Opinion Quarterly* 33, no. 3 (1969): 370–79. https:// doi.org/10.1086/267720

Bergh, Johannes. "Does Voting Rights Affect the Political Maturity of 16-and 17-Year-Olds? Findings from the 2011 Norwegian Voting-Age Trial." *Electoral Studies* 32, no. 1 (2013): 90–100. https://doi.org/10.1016/j.electstud.2012.11.001

Bergh, Johannes, and Jan Eichhorn. "Introduction." In *Lowering the Voting Age to 16: Learning from Real Experiences Worldwide*, edited by Jan Eichhorn and Johannes Berg, 1–12. Palgrave Studies in Young People and Politics. Palgrave Macmillan, 2020.

Bhatti, Yosef, and Kasper M. Hansen. "Leaving the Nest and the Social Act of Voting: Turnout among First-Time Voters." *Journal of Elections, Public Opinion and Parties* 22, no. 4 (November 2012): 380–406. https://www.tandfonline.com/doi/abs/10.1080/17457289.2012.721375

Blais, Andre, Elisabeth Gidengil, and Neil Nevitte. "Where Does Turnout Decline Come From?" *European Journal of Political Research* 43, no. 2 (Fall 2004): 221–36. https://onlinelibrary.wiley.com/doi/full/10.1111/j.1475-6765.2004.00152.x

Blythe, Anne. "Elimination of NC Voter Preregistration Program Creates Confusion for DMV and Elections Officials." *The Charlotte Observer*, July 3, 2014. https://www.charlotteobserver.com/news/politics-government/article9137564.html

Brechenmacher, Saskia. "Comparing Democratic Distress in the United States and Europe." *Carnegie Endowment for International Peace*, June 2018. https://carnegieendowment.org/files/CP_337_Saskia_Full_FINAL.pdf

Brennan, Jan, and Hunter Railey. "The Civics Education Initiative 2015-17." Education Trends. Education Commission of the States, September 2017. https://www.ecs.org/wp-content/uploads/The-Civics-Education-Initiative-2015-2017.pdf

Bright Line Watch. "Bright Line Watch -- Wave 7 Report." Political Survey. Bright Line Watch, November 2018. http://brightlinewatch.org/wave7/

———. "Wave 9 Survey Report." Polling Organization. Bright Line, November 12, 2019. https://brightlinewatch.org/democratic-transgressions-and-constitutional-hardball-bright-line-watch-october-2019-surveys/

Burd, Stephen. "Moving On Up?" *New America*, October 2017, 2–57. https://na-production.s3.amazonaws.com/documents/Moving-on-Up.pdf

Burden, Barry C., David T. Canon, Kenneth R. Mayer, and Donald P. Moynihan. "Election Laws, Mobilization, and Turnout: The Unanticipated Consequences of Election Reform." *American Journal of Political Science* 58, no. 1 (September 9, 2013): 95–109. https://doi.org/10.1111/ajps.12063

Carnevale, Anthony P., Megan L. Fasules, Michael C. Quinn, and Kathryn Peltier Campbell. "Born to Win, Schooled to Lose: Why Equally Talented Students Don't Get Equal Chances to Be All They Can Be." *Georgetown University Center on Education and the Workforce*, 2019. https://cew.georgetown.edu/cew-reports/schooled2lose/

Center for American Women and Politics. *Gender Differences in Voter Turnout*. Eagleton Institute of Politics, Rutgers University, September 16, 2019. https://cawp.rutgers.edu/sites/default/files/resources/genderdiff.pdf

Center for Information & Research on Civic Learning and Engagement. "High School Civics Requirements and Assessments Vary Across the U.S." *Educational. Blog*, June 4, 2014. https://civicyouth.org/high-school-civics-requirements-and-assessments-vary-across-the-u-s/?cat_id=10

Chan, Tak Wing, and Matthew Clayton. "Should the Voting Age Be Lowered to Sixteen? Normative and Empirical Considerations." *Political Studies* 54, no. 3 (2006): 533–58. https://doi.org/10.1111/j.1467-9248.2006.00620.x.

Chua, Amy. *Political Tribes: Group Instinct and the Fate of Nations.* New York, NY: Penguin Press, 2018.

Colby, Anne, Thomas Ehrlich, and Josh Corngold. *Educating for Democracy: Preparing Undergraduates for Responsible Political Engagement.* Stanford, CA: The Carnegie Foundation for the Advancement of Teaching, 2010.

Commission on Youth Voting and Civic Knowledge. "All Together Now: Collaboration and Innovation for Youth Engagement." Equitable K-12 Civic Learning. Center for Information & Research on Civic Learning and Engagement, Tufts University, 2013. https://circle.tufts.edu/sites/default/files/2020-01/all_tog ether_now_commission_report_2013.pdf

Cultice, Wendell W. *Youth's Battle for the Ballot: A History of Voting Age in America.* Contributions in Political Science 291. Westport, CT: Greenwood Press, 1992.

Dahlgaard, Jens Olav. "Trickle Up Political Socialization: The Causal Effect on Turnout of Parenting a Newly Enfranchised Voter." *American Political Science Review* 112, no. 3 (August 2018): 698–705. https://search.proquest.com/docview /2063714620/fulltext/A166888BB14C4704PQ/16?accountid=14968

Dalton, Russel J. *The Good Citizen: How a Younger Generation is Reshaping American Politics.* 2nd ed. Thousand Oaks, CA: CQ Press, 2015.

———. *The Participation Gap: Social Status and Political Inequality.* Oxford, UK: Oxford University Press, 2017.

Dawkins, Richard, and R. Elisabeth Cornwell. "Dodgy Frontal Lobes, y'dig?: The Brain Just Isn't Ready to Vote at 16." *The Guardian*, December 13, 2003. https:// www.theguardian.com/politics/2003/dec/13/highereducation.voterapathy

Desilver, Drew. "U.S. Trails Most Developed Countries in Voter Turnout." Polling Organization. *Pew Research Center*, May 15, 2017. https://static1.squarespace.co m/static/58706fbb29687f06dd219990/t/5b108a8d70a6ad1221aa63c1/152781070 1921/U.S+voter+turnout+lower+than+most+countries+-+Pew+May+2017.pdf

Dinas, Elias. "The Formation of Voting Habits." *Journal of Elections, Public Opinion and Parties* 22, no. 4 (October 2012): 431–56. https://doi.org/10.1080/17457289 .2012.718280

Dottle, Rachael, Ella Koeze, and Julia Wolfe. "The 2018 Midterms, in 4 Charts." Political Analysis. *FiveThrityEight*, November 18, 2018. https://fivethirtyeight.c om/features/the-2018-midterms-in-4-charts/

Douglas, Joshua A. "Lowering the Voting Age from the Ground Up: The United States' Experience in Allowing 16-Year-Olds to Vote." In *Lowering the Voting Age to 16: Learning from Real Experiences Worldwide,* edited by Jan Eichhorn and Johannes Berg, 211–30. Palgrave Studies in Young People and Politics. Palgrave Macmillan, 2020.

Eichhorn, Jan, and Johannes Bergh. "Conclusion." In *Lowering the Voting Age to 16: Learning from Real Experiences Worldwide,* edited by Jan Eichhorn and Johannes Berg, 231–41. Palgrave Studies in Young People and Politics. Palgrave Macmillan, 2020.

————, eds. *Lowering the Voting Age to 16: Learning from Real Experiences Worldwide*. Palgrave Studies in Young People and Politics. Palgrave Macmillan, 2020.

Eichhorn, Jan, Anne Heyer, and Christine Huebner. "Who Influences the Formation of Political Attitudes and Decisions in Young People? Evidence from the Referendum on Scottish Independence." *D Part Think Tank*, April 2014, 13. http://www.poli tischepartizipation.de/images/downloads/2014.03.04_ScottishReferendum_Key% 20Insights_vf.pdf

"Election 2016: Exit Polls." CNN, November 23, 2016. https://www.cnn.com/elect ion/2016/results/exit-polls

Erskine, Hazel. "The Polls: The Politics of Age." *Public Opinion Quarterly* 35, no. 3 (1971): 482–95.

Farkas, Steve, and Ann M. Duffett. "High Schools, Civics, and Citizenship: What Social Studies Teachers Think and Do." American Citizenship. American Enterprise Institute, September 2010. https://www.aei.org/research-products/wo rking-paper/high-schools-civics-and-citizenship/

Fieldhouse, Edward, Mark Tranmer, and Andrew Russell. "Something about Young People or Something about Elections? Electoral Participation of Young People in Europe: Evidence from a Multilevel Analysis of the European Social Survey." *European Journal of Political Research* 46, no. 6 (October 2007): 797–822. https ://doi.org/10.1111/j.1475-6765.2007.00713.x

Flaherty, Colleen. "And Civics Literacy For All." *Inside Higher Ed*, 24 2020, sec. News. https://www.insidehighered.com/news/2020/02/24/purdue-looks-adopt-civi cs-knowledge-undergraduate-requirement?utm_source=Inside+Higher+Ed&utm_ campaign=d4d1bf6aa7-DNU_2019_COPY_02&utm_medium=email&utm_term=0 _1fcbc04421-d4d1bf6aa7-197659373&mc_cid=d4d1bf6aa7&mc_eid=d69009e2ae

Foa, Roberto Stefan, and Yascha Mounk. "The Signs of Deconsolidation." *Journal of Democracy* 28, no. 1 (January 2017): 5–16. https://www.journalofdemocracy.org/ articles/the-signs-of-deconsolidation/

Fraga, Bernard L. *The Turnout Gap: Face, Ethnicity, and Political Inequality in a Diversifying America*. Cambridge, UK: Cambridge University Press, 2018.

Franklin, Mark N. "Consequences of Lowering the Voting Age to 16: Lessons from Comparative Research." In *Lowering the Voting Age to 16: Learning from Real Experiences Worldwide*, edited by Jan Eichhorn and Johannes Berg, 13–41. Palgrave Studies in Young People and Politics. Palgrave Macmillan, 2020.

————. *Voter Turnout and the Dynamics of Electoral Competition in Established Democracies since 1945*. New York, NY: Cambridge University Press, 2004.

Franklin, Mark N., Patrick Lyons, and Michael Marsh. "Generational Basis of Turnout Decline in Established Democracies." *Acta Politica* 39 (2004): 115–51. https://search.proquest.com/docview/217159473?pq-origsite=360link

Freeman, Richard B. "What Do Unions Do.....To Voting?" Working Paper 9992. NBER Working Paper Series. National Bureau of Economic Research, September 2003. https://www.nber.org/papers/w9992

Gallego, Aina. *Unequal Political Participation Worldwide*. New York, NY: Cambridge University Press, 2015.

————. "Where Else Does Turnout Decline Come from? Education, Age, Generation and Period Effects in Three European Countries." *Scandinavian Political Studies* 32, no. 1 (January 2009): 23–44. https://doi.org/10.1111/j.1467-9477.2008.0021 2.x

Global Citizen. Public Interest Organization, n.d. https://www.globalcitizen.org/en/

"Global Democracy in Retreat." Political Analysis. Economist Intelligence Unit: The Economist, January 21, 2020. https://www.eiu.com/n/global-democracy-in -retreat/

Grabenstein, Hannah. "Should 16-Year-Olds Be Allowed to Vote?" News Organization. PBS, April 28, 2018. https://www.pbs.org/newshour/politics/sh ould-16-year-olds-be-allowed-to-vote

Gray, Emma. "Here's What It's Like To Be A Teenage Girl in Alabama Right Now." News. Huffington Post: Women, May 23, 2019. https://www.huffpost.com/entry/ teen-girl-alabama-abortion-ban-jocelyn-wright_n_5ce6a9f6e4b0547bd1337c2e

Green, Donald P., and Ron Schachar. "Habit Formation and Political Behaviour: Evidence of Consuetude in Voter Turnout." *British Journal of Political Science* 30, no. 4 (October 2000): 561–73. https://doi.org/10.1017/S0007123400000247

Hart, Daniel, and Robert Atkins. "American Sixteen-and Seventeen-Year-Olds Are Ready to Vote." *ANNALS of the American Academy of Political and Social Science* 833, no. 1 (2011): 201–22. https://doi.org/10.1177/0002716210382395

Hart, Daniel, and James Youniss. *Renewing Democracy in Young America*. New York, NY: Oxford University Press, 2017.

Haspel, Moshe, and H. Gibbs Knotts. "Location, Location, Location: Precinct Placement and the Costs of Voting." *The Journal of Politics* 67, no. 2 (May 2005): 560–73. https://doi.org/10.1111/j.1468-2508.2005.00329.x

Highton, Benjamin. "Residential Mobility, Community Mobility, and Electoral Participation." *Political Behavior* 22, no. 2 (June 2000): 109–20. https://doi.org/10 .1023/A:1006651130422

Highton, Benjamin, and Raymond E. Woflinger. "Estimating the Effects of the National Voter Registration Act of 1993." *Political Behavior* 20, no. 2 (1998): 79–104. https://doi.org/10.1023/A:1024851912336

Highton, Benjamin, and Raymond E. Wolfinger. "The First Seven Years of the Political Life Cycle." *American Journal of Political Science* 45, no. 1 (2001): 202–9. https://doi.org/https://www.jstor.org/stable/2669367

Hillygus, D. Sunshine. "The Missing Link: Exploring the Relationship Between Higher Education and Political Engagement." *Political Behavior* 27, no. 1 (March, 2005): 25–47. https://doi.org/10.1007/s11109-005-3075-8

Hobbs, William R. "Major Life Events and the Age-Partisan Stability Association." *Political Behavior* 41 (June 7, 2018): 791–814. https://link.springer.com/content/p df/10.1007/s11109-018-9472-6.pdf

Holbein, John B., and D. Sunshine Hillygus. *Making Young Voters: Converting Civic Attitudes into Civic Action*. Cambridge, UK: Cambridge University Press, 2020.

————. "Making Young Voters: The Impact of Preregistration on Youth Turnout." *American Journal of Political Science* 60, no. 2 (April 2016): 364–82.

Huebner, Christine, and Jan Eichhorn. "Votes at 16 in Scotland: Political Experiences Beyond the Vote Itself." In *Lowering the Voting Age to 16: Learning from Real Experiences Worldwide*, edited by Jan Eichhorn and Johannes Berg, 121–42. Palgrave Studies in Young People and Politics. Palgrave Macmillan, 2020.

Jamieson, Kathleen Hall. "The Challenges Facing Civic Education in the 21st Century." *Daedalus* 142, no. 2 (2013): 65–83. https://www.jstor.org/stable /43297234

Johnson, Elin. "Utah to Phase Out Merit Scholarships." *Inside Higher Ed*, Quick Takes, November 25, 2019. https://www.insidehighered.com/quicktakes/2019/11/ 25/utah-phase-out-merit-scholarships#.Xk__V7OZe1A.link

Jones, Stephen R. G. "Was There a Hawthorne Effect?" *American Journal of Sociology* 98, no. 3 (1992): 451–68. https://doi.org/10.1086/230046

Kam, Cindy D., and Carl L Palmer. "Reconsidering the Effects of Education on Political Participation." *Journal of Politics* 70, no. 3 (July 2008): 612–31.

Kaplan, Ethan, and Sharun Mukand. "The Persistence of Political Partisanship: Evidence from 9/11," November 15, 2010. https://warwick.ac.uk/fac/soc/econo mics/staff/swmukand/ideologypersistence11-15.pdf

Kasperowicz, Pete. "House Rejects Democratic Push to Let 16-Year-Olds Vote." *Washington Examiner*, March 7, 2019. https://www.washingtonexaminer.com/ news/house-rejects-democratic-push-to-let-16-year-olds-vote

Kennedy, Robert. "Day of Affirmation Address," June 6, 1966. https://www.jfklibra ry.org/learn/about-jfk/the-kennedy-family/robert-f-kennedy/robert-f-kennedy-spee ches/day-of-affirmation-address-university-of-capetown-capetown-south-africa -june-6-1966

Khazan, Olga. "Argentina Lowers Its Voting Age to 16." *The Washington Post*. n.d., sec. WorldViews. https://www.washingtonpost.com/news/worldviews/wp/2012/11 /01/argentina-voting-age/?utm_term=.28a39cb9ad08

Lahtinen, Hannu, Jani Erola, and Hanna Wass. "Sibling Similarities and the Importance of Parental Socioeconomic Position in Electoral Participation." *Social Forces* soz010 (May 2019). https://doi.org/10.1093/sf/soz010

Larsen, Erik Gahner, Klaus Levinsen, and Ulrik Kjaer. "Democracy for the Youth? The Impact of Mock Elections on Voting Age Attitudes." *Journal of Elections, Public Opinion and Parties* 26, no. 4 (2016): 435–51. https://doi.org/10.1080/1 7457289.2016.1186031

Lawless, Jennifer L., and Richard L. Fox. *Running From Office: Why Young Americans Are Turned off to Politics*. New York, NY: Oxford University Press, 2015.

Leighley, Jan E., and Jonathan Nagler. *Who Votes Now?: Demographics, Issues, Inequality and Turnout in the United States*. Princeton, NJ: Princeton University Press, 2014.

Leininger, Arndt, and Thorsten Faas. "Votes at 16 in Germany: Examining Subnational Variation." In *Lowering the Voting Age to 16: Learning from Real Experiences Worldwide*, edited by Jan Eichhorn and Johannes Berg, 143–66. Palgrave Studies in Young People and Politics. Palgrave Macmillan, 2020.

Levitsky, Steven, and Daniel Ziblatt. *How Democracies Die*. New York, NY: Crown Publishing Group, 2018.

Lichtman, Allan. *The Embattled Vote in America: From the Founding to the Present.* Cambridge, MA: Harvard University Press, 2018.

Lijphart, Arend. "Unequal Participation: Democracy's Unresolved Dilemma." *American Political Science Review* 91, no. 1 (1997): 1–14. https://www.jstor.org/stable/2952255?seq=1#metadata_info_tab_contents

Lopez, German. "7 Specific Ways States Made It Harder for Americans to Vote in 2016." Political. Vox, 07 2016. https://www.vox.com/policy-and-politics/2016/11/7/13545718/voter-suppression-early-voting-2016.\

———. "How the Voting Rights Act Transformed Black Voting Rights in the South, in One Chart." Political Analysis. Vox. Accessed March 13, 2020. https://www.vox.com/2015/3/6/8163229/voting-rights-act-1965

Mackinnon, Amy, and C.K. Hickey. "The Kids Aren't Alright." *Foreign Policy*, May 28, 2019. https://foreignpolicy.com/2019/05/28/us-ranks-with-china-in-child-well-being-save-the-children-end-of-childhood-report-2019/

Malala Yousafzai Biographical. Organizational. The Nobel Prize. Accessed March 7, 2020. https://www.nobelprize.org/prizes/peace/2014/yousafzai/biographical/

Manfedi, Christopher P. "Institutional Design and the Politics of Constitutional Modification: Understanding Failure in the United States and Canada." *Law & Society Review* 31, no. 1 (1997): 111–36. https://www.jstor.org/stable/3054096?seq=1#metadata_info_tab_contents

Mann, Thomas E., and Norman J. Ornstein. *It's Even Worse That It Looks: How the American Constitutional System Collided with the New Politics of Extremism.* New York, NY: Basic Books, 2012.

Marshall, John. "The Anti-Democrat Diploma: How High School Education Decreases Support for the Democratic Party." *American Journal of Political Science* 63, no. 1 (January 2019): 67–83. https://doi.org/10.1111/ajps.12409

Mayhew, Matthew J., and Alyssa N. Rockenbach. "Does College Turn People into Liberals?" The Conversation, February 2, 2016. https://theconversation.com/does-college-turn-people-into-liberals-90905

Mayne, Quinton, and Brigitte Geissel. "Don't Good Democracies Need 'Good' Citizens? Citizen Dispositions and the Study of Democratic Quality." *Politics and Governance* 6, no. 1 (March 2018): 33–47. https://doi.org/10.17645/pag.v6i1.1216

Mazzei, Patricia. "Parkland: A Year After the School Shooting That Was Supposed to Change Everything." *New York Times*, February 13, 2019. https://www.nytimes.com/2019/02/13/us/parkland-anniversary-marjory-stoneman-douglas.html

McAvoy, Paula, Rebecca Fine, and Ann Herrera. *State Standards Scratch the Surface of Learning about Political Parties and Ideology.* K-12 Schools and Civic Education, Center for Information & Research on Civic Learning & Engagement, Tufts University, 2016. https://circle.tufts.edu/sites/default/files/2020-01/WP81_StateStandardsPoliticalIdeoloy_2016.pdf9

McDonald, Michael P. "United States Election Project: Voter Turnout Demographics." Political Data. United States Election Project. Accessed March 7, 2020. http://www.electproject.org/home/voter-turnout/demographics

McDonald, Michael P., and Matthew Thornburg. "Registering the Youth through Voter Preregistration." *New York University Journal of Legislation & Public Policy* 13 (2010): 551–72.

Milkman, Ruth. "A New Political Generation: Millennials and the Post-2008 Wave of Protest." *American Sociological Review* 82, no. 1 (2017): 1–31. https://doi.org /10.1177/0003122416681031

Milner, Henry. *The Internet Generation: Engaged Citizens or Political Dropouts.* Lebanon, NH: Tufts University Press, 2010.

Milner, Henry. "Political Knowledge, Civic Education and Voting at 16." In *Lowering the Voting Age to 16: Learning from Real Experiences Worldwide*, edited by Jan Eichhorn and Johannes Berg, 65–79. Palgrave Studies in Young People and Politics. Palgrave Macmillan, 2020.

"Mission & Story." Political. March for our Lives, n.d. https://marchforourlives.com /mission-story/

Mycock, Andrew, Thomas Loughran, and Jonathan Tonge. "Understanding the Policy Drivers and Effects of Voting Age Reform." In *Lowering the Voting Age to 16: Learning from Real Experiences Worldwide*, edited by Jan Eichhorn and Johannes Berg, 43–63. Palgrave Studies in Young People and Politics. Palgrave Macmillan, 2020.

National Conference of State Legislatures. "Absentee and Early Voting." Non-Profit. NCSL, April 3, 2019. http://www.ncsl.org/research/elections-and-campaigns/ab sentee-and-early-voting.aspx.

Norris, Pippa. "Is Western Democracy Backsliding? Diagnosing the Risks." *Journal of Democracy*, no. April 2017 (n.d.). https://www.journalofdemocracy.org/wp-co ntent/uploads/2018/12/Journal-of-Democracy-Web-Exchange-Norris_0.pdf

North Carolina General Assembly, "Article IX Education," 1971. https://www.ncleg .gov/Laws/Constitution/Article9

Odegard, Guro, Johannes Bergh, and Jo Saglie. "Why Did Young Norwegians Mobilize: External Events or Early Enfranchisement?" In *Lowering the Voting Age to 16: Learning from Real Experiences Worldwide*, 189–210. Palgrave Studies in Young People and Politics. Palgrave Macmillan, 2020.

Orkand, Bob. "I Ain't Got No Quarrel With Them Vietcong." *New York Times*, June 27, 2017, sec. Opinion. https://www.nytimes.com/2017/06/27/opinion/muhammad -ali-vietnam-war.html

Pasek, Josh, Lauren Feldman, Daniel Romer, and Kathleen Hall Jamieson. "Schools as Incubators of Democratic Participation: Building Long-Term Political Efficacy with Civic Education." *Applied Developmental Science* 12, no. 1 (2008): 26–37. https://doi.org/10.1080/10888690801910526

Perrin, Andrew J., and Alanna Gillis. "How College Makes Citizens: Higher Education Experiences and Political Engagement." *Socius: Sociological Research for a Dynamic World* 5 (2019): 1–16. https://doi.org/10.1177/2378023119859708

Perry, Douglas. "Oregon Lawmakers Seek to Lower Voting Age in State to 16, so Teens Can 'Protect Their Future.'" News Organization. The Oregonian/ OregonLive, February 19, 2019. https://www.oregonlive.com/politics/2019/02/o regon-lawmakers-seek-to-lower-voting-age-in-state-to-16-so-teens-can-protect-the ir-future.html

Persson, Mikael. "Education and Political Participation." *British Journal of Political Science* 45, no. 3 (July 2015): 689–703. https://doi.org/10.1017/S0007123413 000409

Petraca, Constanza Sanhueza. "Does Voting at a Younger Age Have an Effect on Satisfaction with Democracy and Political Trust? Evidence from Latin America." In *Lowering the Voting Age to 16: Learning from Real Experiences Worldwide*, 103–19. Palgrave Studies in Young People and Politics. Palgrave Macmillan, 2020.

Pew Research Center. "After Seismic Political Shift, Modest Changes in Public's Policy Agenda." Research Organization. Pew Research Center, January 24, 2017. https://www.people-press.org/2017/01/24/after-seismic-political-shift-modest-cha nges-in-publics-policy-agenda/

———. "Public Opinion on Abortion: Views on Abortion 1995-2019." Polling Organization. Religion and Public Life, August 29, 2019. https://www.pewforum .org/fact-sheet/public-opinion-on-abortion/

———. "The Party of Nonvoters." U.S. Politics & Policy. Pew Research Center, October 31, 2014. https://www.people-press.org/2014/10/31/the-party-of-nonvote rs-2/

———. "The Public, the Political System and American Democracy." Polling Organization. Pew Research Center, April 28, 2018. https://www.people-press.org /2018/04/26/the-public-the-political-system-and-american-democracy/

Pfeffer, Fabian T. "Persistent Inequality in Educational Attainment and Its Institutional Context." *European Sociological Review* 24, no. 5 (May 2008): 543–65. https:// www.jstor.org/stable/25209187

Plutzer, Eric. "Becoming a Habitual Voter: Inertia, Resources, and Growth in Young Adulthood." *American Political Science Review* 96, no. 1 (March 2002): 41–56. https://doi.org/10.1017/S0003055402004227

Popken, Ben. "Only 37 Percent of Americans Think Their Kids Will Be Better Off." News. NBC News, June 6, 2017. https://www.nbcnews.com/business/consumer/ only-37-percent-americans-think-their-kids-will-be-better-n768706

"Public Support 'the Right to Vote at 16' More than 'Reducing the Voting Age from 18 to 16.'" Polling Organization. YouGov, n.d. https://yougov.co.uk/topics/politic s/articles-reports/2018/05/23/public-support-right-vote-16-more-reducing-voting-

Rafa, Alyssa, Dave Rogowski, Hunter Railey, Paul Baumann, and Stephanie Aragon. "50-State Comparison: Civic Education Policies." Research & Reports. Education Commission of the States, December 12, 2016. https://www.ecs.org/citizenship -education-policies/

Rakich, Nathaniel. "What Happened When 2.2 Million People Were Automatically Registered to Vote." Polling Organization. 538 Politics: Voting, October 10, 2019. https://fivethirtyeight.com/features/what-happened-when-2-2-million-people- were-automatically-registered-to-vote/?utm_source=pocket-newtab

Rawls, John. *A Theory of Justice*. Revised. Cambridge, MA: Harvard University Press, 1999.

"Reelection Rates Over the Years." Politicians & Elections. OpenSecrets.org: Center for Responsive Politics. Accessed February 14, 2020. https://www.opensecrets.org /overview/reelect.php

Rimmerman, Craig A. *The New Citizenship: Unconventional Politics, Activism, and Service.* Boulder, CO: Westview, 1998.

Roberts, Sam. "The Port Huron Statement at 50." *New York Times*, March 3, 2012, sec. New Analysis. https://www.nytimes.com/2012/03/04/sunday-review/the-port-huron-statement-at-50.html

Rojanasakul, Mira, Jeremy C. F. Lin, Lauren Leatherby, Alison McCartney, Demetrios Pogkas, and David Ingold. "Americans Actually Voted in the 2018 Midterms." *Bloomberg*, December 20, 2018. https://www.bloomberg.com/graphics/2018-midterm-election-turnout-shifts/

Russell, Andrew. "The Case for Lowering the Voting Age Is Less Persuasive Now than at Any Point in the Last 50 Years." Political. Democraticaudit.com, May 16, 2014. https://www.democraticaudit.com/2014/05/16/highlighting-the-minimal-rights-accrued-by-16-year-olds-is-a-flawed-argument-for-lowering-the-voting-age/

Schaeffer, Katherine. "Share of Americans Who Favor Stricter Gun Laws Has Increased since 2017." Research Organization. Pew Research Center, October 16, 2019. https://www.pewresearch.org/fact-tank/2019/10/16/share-of-americans-who-favor-stricter-gun-laws-has-increased-since-2017/

Schaffer, Frederic Charles. *The Hidden Costs of Clean Election Reform.* Ithaca, NY: Cornell University, 2008.

Schattschneider, Elmer Eric. *The Semi-Sovereign People: A Realist's View of Democracy in America.* Boston, MA: Wadsworth, 1960.

Shapiro, Sarah, and Catherine Brown. "The State of Civics Education." Education, K-12. Center for American Progress, February 21, 2018. https://www.americanprogress.org/issues/education-k-12/reports/2018/02/21/446857/state-civics-education/

Shelbourne, Mallory. "Poll: Kim Jong Un Has Higher Approval among Republicans than Pelosi." *The Hill*, June 18, 2018. https://thehill.com/homenews/house/392756-poll-kim-jong-un-has-higher-approval-among-republicans-than-pelosi

Solt, Frederick. "Economic Inequality and Democratic Political Engagement." *American Journal of Political Science* 52, no. 1 (January 2008): 48–60. https://doi.org/10.1111/j.1540-5907.2007.00298.x

Sondheimer, Rachel Milstein, and Donald P. Green. "Using Experiments to Estimate the Effects of Education on Voter Turnout." *American Journal of Political Science* 54, no. 1 (January 2010): 174–89. https://doi.org/pdf/10.1111/j.1540-5907.2009.00425.x

St. Amour, Madeline. "New Grant Program at Pitt Matches Pell Grants and Targets Students' Unmet Need." *Inside Higher Ed*, October 18, 2019. https://www.insidehighered.com/print/news/2019/10/18/new-grant-program-pitt-matches-pell-grants-and-targets-students-unmet-need

"State Laws Governing Early Voting." Government. National Conference of State Legislatures, August 2, 2019. https://www.ncsl.org/research/elections-and-campaigns/early-voting-in-state-elections.aspx

"State of the News Media." Polling Organization. Digital News Fact Sheet, n.d. https://www.journalism.org/fact-sheet/digital-news/

"Status and Trends in the Education of Racial and Ethnic Groups." Data. Institute of Education Sciences: National Center for Education Statistics, February 2019. https ://nces.ed.gov/programs/raceindicators/indicator_RAA.asp

Sunstein, Cass, ed. *Can It Happen Here? Authoritarianism in America.* New York, NY: Dey St., 2018.

Tamas, Bernard. "American Disproportionality: A Historical Analysis of Partisan Bias in Elections to the U.S. House of Representatives." *Election Law Journal* 18, no. 1 (2019): 47–62. https://doi.org/10.1089/elj.2017.0464

The Economist Intelligence Unit. "Democracy Index 2018: Me Too?: Political Participation, Protest, and Democracy." Democracy Index, n.d. http://www.eiu. com/Handlers/WhitepaperHandler.ashx?fi=Democracy_Index_2018.pdf&mode =wp&campaignid=Democracy2018

The Editors. "A School Is Not a Military Post." *Scientific American*, January 2018. https://www.scientificamerican.com/article/a-call-to-make-schools-safe-zones-not -war-zones/

Toots, Anu, and Tonu Idnurm. "Modernizing Voting in a Post-Transition Country: The Estonian Experience of Lowering the Voting Age." In *Lowering the Voting Age to 16: Learning from Real Experiences Worldwide*, 167–87. Palgrave Studies in Young People and Politics. Palgrave Macmillan, 2020.

Tucker, Patrick D., Jacob M. Montgomery, and Steven S. Smith. "Party Identification in the Age of Obama: Evidence on the Sources of Stability and Systematic Change in Party Identification from a Long-Term Panel Survey." *Political Research Quarterly* 72, no. 2 (2019): 309–28. https://doi.org/10.1177/1065912918784215

Uggen, Christopher, Ryan Larson, and Sarah Shannon. "6 Million Lost Voters: State-Level Estimates of Felony Disenfranchisement, 2016." *The Sentencing Project*, October 6, 2016. https://www.sentencingproject.org/publications/6-million-lost -voters-state-level-estimates-felony-disenfranchisement-2016/

U.S. Department of Education. "Beginning College Students Who Change Their Majors Within 3 Years of Enrollment." Data Point, December 2017. https://nces .ed.gov/pubs2018/2018434.pdf

Vasilogambros, Matt. "Thousands Lose Right to Vote Under 'Incompetence' Laws." News. Stateline, March 21, 2018. https://www.pewtrusts.org/en/research-and-ana lysis/blogs/stateline/2018/03/21/thousands-lose-right-to-vote-under-incompetence -laws

"Voter Friendly Campus." Education. Voter Friendly Campus, October 2019. https:// www.voterfriendlycampus.org/

"Voter Turnout Database." Data. International IDEA. Accessed March 8, 2020. https ://www.idea.int/data-tools/data/voter-turnout

"Voting in Primaries at 17 Years Old." News Organization. Ballotpedia, April 30, 2019. https://ballotpedia.org/Voting_in_primaries_at_17_years_old

Wagner, Markus, David Johann, and Sylvia Kritzinger. "Voting at 16: Turnout and the Quality of Vote Choice." *Electoral Studies* 31, no. 2 (2012): 372–83. https://do i.org/10.1016/j.electstud.2012.01.007

Wattenberg, Martin. *Is Voting for Young People?* 4th ed. New York, NY: Routledge, 2016.

Bibliography

Woods, Randall B. "The Politics of Idealism: Lyndon Johnson, Civil Rights, and Vietnam." *Diplomatic History* 31, no. 1 (December 11, 2006): 1–18. https://doi.org /10.1111/j.1467-7709.2007.00599.x

Woodward, C. Vann. *The Strange Career of Jim Crow*. 3rd ed. Oxford: Oxford University Press, 1974.

Yang 2020. "Policy: Lower the Voting Age to 16." Political Campaign. Yang 2020, n.d. https://www.yang2020.com/policies/votingage/

"Young People's Ambivalent Relationship with Political Parties." Data Analysis. Center for Information & Research on Civic Learning and Engagement: Tufts University, October 24, 2018. https://circle.tufts.edu/latest-research/young-peo ples-ambivalent-relationship-political-parties

Zakaria, Fareed. "The Rise of Illiberal Democracy." *Foreign Affairs* 76, no. 6 (December 1997): 22–43. https://www.foreignaffairs.com/articles/1997-11-01/rise -illiberal-democracy

Zeglovits, Eva, and Julian Aichholzer. "Are People More Inclined to Vote at 16 than at 18? Evidence for the First-Time Voting Boost among 16-to 25-Year-Olds in Austria." *Journal of Elections, Public Opinion and Parties* 24, no. 3 (2014): 351–63. https://doi.org/10.1080/17457289.2013.872652

Zeglovits, Eva, and Martina Zandonella. "Political Interest of Adolescents before and after Lowering the Vote Age: The Case of Austria." *Journal of Youth Studies* 16, no. 8 (2013): 1084–1104. https://doi.org/10.1080/13676261.2013.793785

Index

About the Author

Trained in Political Science at the University of North Carolina at Chapel Hill, **Niall Guy Michelsen** began his professional career at Roosevelt University (Chicago) from 1989 to 2001. He has been teaching at Western Carolina University since 2001. There, he has fulfilled several administrative roles, including department chair, associate dean, and director of international studies. He has published scholarly articles and book chapters on the scholarship of teaching and learning, international politics, specifically on nuclear issues and issues of international cooperation and conflict. He regularly teaches courses on US Foreign Policy, Political Theory, and Global Issues. He participated in the Japan Studies Institute at San Diego State University in 2014 and traveled to Japan with the Japan Studies Institute in 2015. He also traveled to China with the China Studies Institute in 2017. He has been actively involved with the American Democracy Project that is sponsored by the American Association of State Colleges and Universities.